Solutions

Pre-Intermediate Workbook

Tim Falla, Paul A Davie

OXFORD
UNIVERSITY PRESS

OXFORD
UNIVERSITY PRESS

Great Clarendon Street, Oxford OX2 6DP

Oxford University Press is a department of the University of Oxford.
It furthers the University's objective of excellence in research, scholarship,
and education by publishing worldwide in

Oxford New York

Auckland Cape Town Dar es Salaam Hong Kong Karachi
Kuala Lumpur Madrid Melbourne Mexico City Nairobi
New Delhi Shanghai Taipei Toronto

With offices in

Argentina Austria Brazil Chile Czech Republic France Greece
Guatemala Hungary Italy Japan Poland Portugal Singapore
South Korea Switzerland Thailand Turkey Ukraine Vietnam

OXFORD and OXFORD ENGLISH are registered trade marks of
Oxford University Press in the UK and in certain other countries

© Oxford University Press 2008

The moral rights of the author have been asserted

Database right Oxford University Press (maker)

First published 2008
2017 2016 2015 2014
20 19 18 17

No unauthorized photocopying

All rights reserved. No part of this publication may be reproduced,
stored in a retrieval system, or transmitted, in any form or by any means, without
the prior permission in writing of Oxford University Press,
or as expressly permitted by law, or under terms agreed with the appropriate
reprographics rights organization. Enquiries concerning reproduction outside
the scope of the above should be sent to the ELT Rights Department, Oxford
University Press, at the address above

You must not circulate this book in any other binding or cover
and you must impose this same condition on any acquirer

Any websites referred to in this publication are in the public domain and their
addresses are provided by Oxford University Press for information only. Oxford
University Press disclaims any responsibility for the content

ISBN: 978 0 19 4551700

Printed in China

ACKNOWLEDGEMENTS

*The publisher and authors are very grateful to the many teachers and students who read
and piloted the manuscript, and provided invaluable feedback. With special thanks to*
Hana Musílková (Czech Republic), Eva Paulerová (Czech Republic), Dagmar
Škorpíková (Czech Republic), Danica Gondová (Slovakia), Nyírő Zsuzsanna
(Hungary), Elekes Katalin (Hungary), Kelemen Ferenc (Hungary), Rézműves Zoltán
(Hungary), Nataska Koltko (Ukraine), Zinta Andžāne (Latvia), Irena Budreikiene
(Lithuania) *for their contribution to the development of the Solutions series.*

Additional materials by: James Gault *and* Małgorzata Wieruszewska

*The authors and publisher are grateful to those who have given permission to reproduce
the following extracts and adaptations of copyright material*:
p38 'Every Day is Sunday Here' by Michele Hanson. Copyright © Michele Hanson
2006. p39 'Author Interview: Gap Years for Grown Ups' reproduced with permission of
www.gapyear.com p48 'Galapagos' by K. Morgenstern www.sacredearth-travel.com.
Reproduced with permission. p48 'Galapagos National Park Rules' reproduced with
permission of www.galapagosonline.com. p58 'Tips to Protect Yourself While Shopping
Online' © 2006 by Marcy Zitz. Used with permission of About, Inc., which can be found
online at www.about.com. All Rights Reserved. p68 'Boycott or No, Students Get
Results' by Peter C. Beller. From The New York Times, 10 April 2005 © 2005 The New
York Times All Rights Reserved. Used by permission and protected by the Copyright
Laws of the United States. The printing, copying, redistribution, or retransmission of the
Material without express written permission is prohibited. p78 'Angela's Diary Entries'
by Angela Kidson. Reproduced with permission of www.volunteersforalaska.org. p88
'A Musical Career Gap' reproduced with permission of www.gapyear.com. p94 'Author
Interview: Philip Pullman', reproduced with permission of Philip Pullman and
Scholastic Limited. All Rights Reserved. p107 '£1.25 BN Worth of Gadgets Never Even
get out of the Box' Evening Standard's www.thislondon.co.uk. Reproduced with kind
permission of Solo Syndication.

Although every effort has been made to trace and contact copyright holders before
publication, this has not been possible in some cases. We apologize for any apparent
infringement of copyright and if notified, the publisher will be pleased to rectify any
errors or omissions at the earliest opportunity.

Sources:
www.vivatravelguides.com

Illustrations by:
Jonas Bergstrand/CIA pp17, 23, 33, 60 (P.E), 61, 67, 83 (DVD shop), 91, 92
Claude Bordeleau/Agent 002 pp7, 13, 15, 16, 43, 48, 51, 53, 60, 63, 71, 73, 75, 81, 83
(scenarios); 86; Jean-Luc Guerin/Comillus p93; David Oakley/Arnos Design Ltd pp30,
59, 70, 90 (cover and contents page), 109 (Joanna); Fred Van Deelen/Rebecca Hall/The
Organisation pp9, 12, 19, 22, 26, 27, 45, 85, 90 (14 book covers), 95

*The Publisher would like to thank the following for their permission to reproduce
photographs*:
Action Plus pp6 (skateboarding, horse riding), 18 (Muhammed Ali/Manny Millan/Icon),
105 (Paula Radcliffe); Alamy p41, 55 (girl on phone), 76 (James Bartholomew), 79
(recycling/Helene Rogers), (protest/David Hoffman Photo Library), 108 (David Ball);
Apple p50 (ipods); Arnos Design Ltd pp50 (DVD player, calculator, TV, CD player), 72
(plastic bag), 80 (novelist); Camera Press p18 (Nadia Komaneci/Ullstein Rzepka);
Cannon p50 (camcorder); Corbis pp6 (karate), 10 (Mandy/Kate Mitchell/Zefa),
(Tom/Rick Barrentine), 18 (Lance Armstrong/ Elizabeth Kreutz), (Martina Navratilova/
Reuters), (Pele/Hulton-Deutsch Collection), 23 (New York), 28 (Oxford/Eric Narthan/
Loop Images), 31, 39 (woman on mobile phone/ R.Wright), 64, 107 (sat nav/Najlah
Feanny), 109 (Elizabeth Whiting & Associates); Empics p14 (John Giles); Getty Images
pp6 (band/ Yellow Dog Productions), 8 (goth), 18 (Ferenc Puskas/STF/AFP, (Katarina
Witt/David Cannon), (Johnson/Sean Garnsworthy), 24 (Derek Lebowski), 28
(Snowdonia/David Noton), 39 (woman using payphone/Paul Thomas), 43, 50, 55 (boy
on phone), 72 (crop spraying/Chuck Keeler/Stone), 80 (artist, politician, violinist,
photographer); Istockphoto/Juan Manimo p69 (waitress), London Features Int. p80
(singer); Merlin Entertainments p107 (aquarium); Nokia p50 (mobile phone); OUP
Classet pp25, 45, 69 (girl with horse), 105 (au pair), 106 (cottage); PA Photos p18 (Tanni
Grey Thompson/Gareth Copley); PURE p50 (digital radio); PYMCA p8 (townies/
Josephine Soughan and Simon Pentle); Random House p96; Rex Features Ltd pp8
(hoody, punk), 13, 34, 42, 44, 48 (stereo, games console, video recorder/Neil
Stevenson), 54, 59 (choir/ITV), 62, 82 (car), 93; Science Photo Library pp72 (sun, oil
platform, land-fill site), 74; The Kobal Collection pp32, 36 (At World's End/ Walt
Disney), 106 (Spiderman 3/Marvel/Sony Pictures; The Marymass Festival and Irvine
Carter's Society p68; Sony p50 (hard disk recorder)

Cover image: Corbis

Wherever you see this symbol, you will find interactive practice in the corresponding section of the MultiROM.

A VOCABULARY AND LISTENING
Personalities

I can describe someone's personality.

1 Find the opposites of these personality adjectives in the word square (↓ and →).

1 ~~confident~~   6 polite
2 hard-working   7 quiet
3 mean   8 serious
4 optimistic   9 unfriendly
5 patient   10 unkind

I	M	P	A	T	I	E	N	T	O
F	R	E	P	A	F	I	K	A	P
D	I	S	R	G	R	G	S	L	T
U	N	S	E	E	U	O	H	K	U
F	R	I	E	N	D	L	Y	A	H
U	M	M	K	E	E	A	H	T	X
N	E	I	Q	R	D	Z	E	I	S
N	A	S	U	O	F	Y	R	V	R
Y	G	T	I	U	C	O	N	E	N
L	Q	I	F	S	E	K	I	N	D
S	E	C	U	N	K	H	Y	U	L

2 Use the adjectives from the word square to complete the sentences.

1 It was very __kind__ of you to help me with my homework.
2 She's a bit _____. That's why she didn't talk to many people at the party.
3 It's _____ to talk with your mouth full.
4 Sally isn't very _____. She prefers to listen to other people.
5 Mark is very _____. He always thinks things will get worse!
6 All the students were very _____ towards me on my first day at my new school.
7 She is too _____ to help me with the housework.
8 Harry's very _____. He's always telling jokes.
9 After waiting over half an hour for the bus, Ben began to get _____.
10 It was very _____ of you to pay for my coffee.

●●●●● **Extension:** Negative prefixes: *un-*, *im-* / *in-* and *dis-*.

3 Make the adjectives negative by adding the correct prefix: *un-*, *dis-*, *in-* or *im-*.

1 comfortable   __uncomfortable__
2 honest   _____
3 fit   _____
4 polite   _____
5 tidy   _____
6 lucky   _____
7 loyal   _____
8 tolerant   _____

4 Use the adjectives in exercise 3, with or without their prefixes, to complete the sentences.

1 I couldn't sleep because the bed was __uncomfortable__.
2 Pete's very _____. He goes running every evening.
3 In many countries it's _____ to start eating before others are ready.
4 His bedroom is always _____ – he never puts anything away.
5 We should be _____ of people who have different religions and beliefs from us.
6 She's very _____. She wouldn't lie to you.
7 John was in a terrible car accident last week. He's _____ to be alive.
8 It was _____ of your friend to say bad things about you when you weren't there.

5 Make a mind map of words that describe personality.

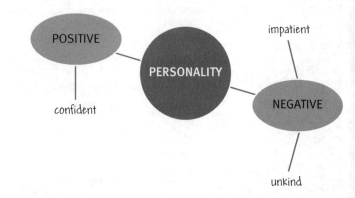

 Extra Practice

1B GRAMMAR
Present simple and continuous

I can say what I usually do and what I'm doing now.

1 Some of the verbs in these sentences are incorrect. Correct them if necessary.

1 'What <u>are you doing</u>?' 'I'm a teacher.'   ✗
   'What do you do?' 'I'm a teacher.'

2 Look. That girl is smiling at you.   ☐
_____

3 He<u>'s going</u> to the gym every day.   ☐
_____

4 I <u>wear</u> jeans today.   ☐
_____

5 I<u>'m not understanding</u> you.   ☐
_____

6 I <u>don't like</u> classical music.   ☐
_____

7 What <u>does she do</u> tomorrow evening?   ☐
_____

8 Which <u>do you prefer</u>, pizza or pasta?   ☐
_____

2 Mario and Sarah are at a dance. Complete the conversation with the verbs in the box. Use the present simple or present continuous.

~~come~~ do have like stay study want work not work

Mario Hi. I'm Mario.

Sarah Hi, I'm Sarah. Where ¹___*do*___ you ___*come*___ from, Péter?

Mario Croatia. I ²_____ with a family here in Brighton.

Sarah ³_____ you _____ it here?

Mario Yes, it's a nice town. I ⁴_____ a great time.

Sarah Your English is very good.

Mario Thanks. I ⁵_____ at a language school. What ⁶_____ you _____, Sarah?

Sarah I'm a nurse.

Mario That's interesting.

Sarah I usually ⁷_____ at night, but I ⁸_____ this evening.

Mario ⁹_____ you _____ to dance?

Sarah OK.

CHALLENGE!

Write two sentences for each use.

Present simple: something that happens always or regularly

1 _____

2 _____

Present continuous: something that's happening now

3 _____

4 _____

Present continuous: arrangements in the future

5 This evening _____

6 After school tomorrow _____

3 Decide whether the present continuous is being used (a) for something that is happening now or (b) for an arrangement in the future. Write *a* or *b*.

1 What are you doing tomorrow night? ___

2 It's starting to rain. ___

3 'Are you planning to stay at home this weekend?' ___ 'No, we're visiting friends in London.' ___

4 Penny is wearing a pink skirt. ___

5 'Where's Wendy?' 'She's reading upstairs.' ___

6 Is Ann coming to the cinema with us this evening? ___

7 I can't meet you on Saturday. I'm playing football. ___

8 My aunt is coming to see us this afternoon. ___

9 What's that music you're listening to? ___

10 What are you wearing to Tom's party? ___

4 Look at Neil's diary and complete the conversation. Use the present continuous.

SATURDAY

3 pm Football – Chelsea v Arsenal
Cinema – 'War of the Worlds' meet Becky at 8 at pizza café

Neil I ¹_____ (watch) a football match on Saturday.

Kate Oh? Who ²_____ (play)?

Neil Chelsea and Arsenal. Why don't you come round and watch it with me?

Kate I don't like football. What ³_____ you _____ (do) in the evening?

Neil I ⁴_____ (go) to the cinema.

Kate Who ⁵_____ you _____ (go) with?

Neil Becky. Do you want to come?

Kate Yes, I'd love to. What time ⁶_____ you and Becky _____ (meet)?

Neil Eight o'clock at the pizza café.

Kate OK. See you there.

Revision: Student's Book page 6

1 Complete the phrases. Use the words in the box.

> chess   computer games   magazines   ~~music~~
> swimming   sport   the Internet
> to an aerobics class   TV   volleyball

1 listen to ___music___
2 watch _____
3 play _____
4 play _____
5 play _____
6 go _____
7 go _____
8 read _____
9 do _____
10 surf _____

2 Read the texts and match them with the pictures.

Sarah ☐

I love animals. I've got four pets – a cat, a dog and two goldfish. Horses are my favourite animal. I go riding every weekend.

Martin ☐

I don't like doing sport very much, but I like watching football on TV. My favourite hobby is playing the guitar. My friends and I have got a band called Fusion. We practise together every Friday evening.

Ben ☐

I've got lots of hobbies. I love computer games and I like watching films on TV or at the cinema. I also like playing chess. I don't do much sport, but I often go rollerblading with my friends.

Vanessa ☐

I love sport. I play volleyball at school and I sometimes go swimming with my sister at the weekend. But my favourite sport is judo. I go to a judo club three times a week.

3 Are the sentences true or false? Write T or F.

1 Sarah has got a horse. ____
2 Sarah goes riding every weekend. ____
3 Martin likes playing football. ____
4 Martin plays guitar in a band. ____
5 Vanessa does three different sports. ____
6 Vanessa's favourite sport is judo. ____
7 Ben hates watching films. ____
8 Ben doesn't get any exercise. ____

4 Answer the questions about your hobbies and interests.

1 What's your favourite hobby?
_____
_____
_____

2 Where do you do it, and who do you do it with?
_____
_____
_____

3 What sports do you like?
_____
_____
_____

●●●●● CHALLENGE! ●●●●●

Complete the sentences with one of these prepositions: *in, on, to, with*. Tick ✓ the sentences that are true for you.

1 I do a lot of sport ___in___ my free time. ☐
2 I sometimes listen to music _____ my own. ☐
3 I'm addicted _____ computer games. ☐
4 Football is more popular _____ boys than girls. ☐
5 I spend a lot of money _____ CDs. ☐
6 I'm very interested _____ computers. ☐
7 I'm not very keen _____ physical exercise. ☐

GRAMMAR
verb + infinitive or *-ing* form

I can identify and use different verb patterns.

1 Complete the sentences. Use the *-ing* form of the verbs in the box.

> copy   get up   ~~go~~   have   help   live   play   think   watch

1 Do you fancy __going__ to the cinema this evening?
2 I spend a lot of time _____ computer games.
3 The food in the school canteen is terrible, so I avoid _____ lunch there.
4 I can't help _____ that he isn't telling the truth.
5 I don't mind _____ my parents with the housework.
6 I can't stand _____ early in the morning.
7 Bob suggested _____ a DVD.
8 Can you imagine _____ in a foreign country?
9 It's really annoying – he keeps _____ my homework.

2 Complete the sentences, using the infinitive form of the verbs in the box. Then match the sentences to the pictures.

> ~~be~~   buy   carry   let   pay   study

1 Kate wants __to be__ a nurse when she leaves school.
2 Tina's parents agreed _____ her go to a rock concert.
3 Harry decided not _____ a new DVD player. They're too expensive.
4 Jake broke the window, but he refused _____ for a new one.
5 Liz is pretending _____ – but she's really listening to music on her MP3 player.
6 Ben offered _____ my suitcase as it was really heavy.

3 Complete the sentences. Use the correct form of the verbs in brackets.

1 Tom offered __to help__ me with my homework. (help)
2 We spent an hour _____ on the phone. (chat)
3 I can't stand _____ a jacket and tie. (wear)
4 He refused _____ his mum where he was going. (tell)
5 He pretended not _____ me. (hear)
6 We decided _____ to Majorca this summer. (go)
7 She can't help _____ nervous about the exams. (feel)
8 I don't fancy _____ tonight. Let's go out. (stay in)
9 I hope _____ you next weekend. (see)
10 I can't imagine _____ old. (be)
11 What time do you expect _____ in London? (arrive)
12 I don't mind _____ football on TV. (watch)
13 Why do you keep _____ that song? It's annoying. (sing)
14 I didn't want to go to the party on my own, so my sister agreed _____ with me. (come)

4 Underline four *-ing* forms and four infinitive forms in the e-mail. Some of them are incorrect. Correct them.

Hi Jackie

How are you? I keep <u>to phone</u> you, but   __phoning__
you're always out, so I decided sending you   _____
an e-mail. I'm having a very boring week. I
spend all my time studying for the exams,
but I refuse to work all weekend, too! So   _____
do you fancy to go to the cinema with me   _____
on Saturday? There are several good films
on that I want to see. I don't mind   _____
seeing any of them, so you can choose.   _____

I hope hearing from you soon.   _____

Lots of love,

William

● ● ● ● ● ● **CHALLENGE!** ● ● ● ● ● ●

Write sentences using these verbs and either the *-ing* form, or the infinitive.

1 can't help __I can't help thinking about the exams.__
2 can't stand _____
3 want _____
4 agree _____
5 hope _____
6 avoid _____

 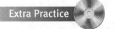

Revision: Student's Book page 8

1 Complete the text with the words in the box.

> agree allowed to bans behave fashion
> fashionable generation gap head teacher ~~rule~~
> unfair uniform

There's a ¹ __rule__ at our school that ² _____ people from wearing hooded tops. I think it's really ³ _____ . We don't have to wear a school ⁴ _____ – we can wear ⁵ _____ clothes and jewellery, so why aren't we⁶ _____ wear hooded tops? Hooded tops are an important part of teenage ⁷ _____ . The ⁸ _____ , Mr Brown, thinks that people who wear hooded tops ⁹ _____ badly. But I don't ¹⁰ _____ . Mr Brown is quite old. There's a ¹¹ _____ between him and the students.

2 Read the text quickly and label the photos with the words in the box.

> goth punk skater hip-hopper

3 Read the text again. Find:

1 two things that hip-hoppers wear.
_____ and _____

2 two things that skaters wear.
_____ and _____

3 two styles of music that goths listen to.
_____ and _____

4 two groups who sometimes have coloured hair.
_____ and _____

5 two bands that skaters listen to.
_____ and _____

6 two groups who often wear make-up.
_____ and _____

7 two styles of music that hip-hoppers listen to.
_____ and _____

4 Complete the sentence. Use *present continuous* or *present simple*.

All the verbs in the text are in the _____ because they describe actions that happen regularly or facts that are always true.

●●●●● **CHALLENGE!** ●●●●●

Write a short paragraph (about 30 words) about (a) or (b).

a The clothes that you like to wear:
  Why do you like them? Do your friends wear similar clothes? What do your parents / teachers think of your clothes?

b The clothes that a group of young people in your country likes to wear:
  Does the group have a name? Do people judge them from the clothes they wear? What kind of music do they like?

Teenage fashions in the UK

Young people sometimes get angry when adults judge their personalities from the clothes they wear. However, young people often do exactly the same thing when they see other young people. They don't look at a person and imagine what they are really like. Instead, they look at their clothes and behaviour and immediately put them into a group. The four most common groups are: skaters, goths, hip-hoppers and punks.

Skaters wear baggy, casual clothes: jeans and hooded tops. They have long hair and sometimes it's coloured. They listen to bands like Green Day, Blink 182, The Offspring and Sum 41.

Goths like to wear black. They're usually quiet people – much quieter than hip-hoppers. They like rock or heavy metal music, not pop music. They often have black hair and make-up.

Hip-hoppers wear sports clothes: smart tracksuits and expensive trainers. They wear baseball caps and often jewellery too. They usually listen to hip hop and rap.

Punks wear old torn clothes. They have coloured hair and often wear make-up and jewellery – but it's often safety pins or rings in their noses, lips or even tongues.

However, some teenagers think that these fashions are silly and that it's better to be an individual than to belong to a group.

1

2

3

4

EVERYDAY ENGLISH

Giving an opinion

I can express my likes and dislikes.

1 Label the pictures. Use the words in the box.

> chatting online dancing doing sport drawing
> going out with friends listening to music
> playing chess playing computer games reading
> shopping taking photos watching TV

 1 <u>chatting online</u>
 2 _____
 3 _____

 4 _____
 5 _____
 6 _____

 7 _____
 8 _____
 9 _____

 10 _____
 11 _____
 12 _____

● ● ● ● ● CHALLENGE! ● ● ● ● ●

How many more hobbies and interests can you add?

1 _____   5 _____
2 _____   6 _____
3 _____   7 _____
4 _____   8 _____

---

2 Match the phrases with the same meanings.

1 Do you fancy …   a I really like …
2 I'd rather …   b I really don't like …
3 I love …   c I prefer …
4 I can't stand …   d Would you like to …

3 Write a sentence using each of the phrases 1–4 from exercise 2.

1 _____
2 _____
3 _____
4 _____

4 Choose the best reply.

1 I like playing chess.
  A Me too. ☐
  B Good idea. ☐

2 I'd rather go swimming.
  A Do you? ☐
  B Really? ☐

3 I enjoy taking photos.
  A So do I. ☐
  B Sure! ☐

4 Do you fancy dancing?
  A Sure. Good idea. ☐
  B So do I. ☐

5 Put the words in the correct order to make questions. Then write true answers.

1 you / your / do / what / in / doing / time / free / like / ?

_____

_____

2 doing / do / you / what / like / else / ?

_____

_____

6 Write the lines in the correct order to make a dialogue.

Ann   Do you? I can't stand playing computer games.
        Really? I prefer Keane. What else do you like doing?
        So do I. What's your favourite band?
        ~~What do you like doing in your free time?~~

Jeremy I like playing computer games.
        I love listening to music.
        The Arctic Monkeys.

Ann <u>What do you like doing in your free time?</u>
Jeremy <u>I love</u> _____
Ann _____
Jeremy _____
Ann _____
Jeremy _____
Ann _____

7 Write a dialogue like the one in exercise 6. Use the information in the chart.

	Sue	Rob
watching sport	☺ Favourite: football	☺ Favourite: rugby
shopping	☺	☹

Rob _____
Sue _____
Rob _____
Sue _____
Rob _____
Sue _____
Rob _____

1G WRITING
A personal profile

I can write a personal profile for an Internet chatroom.

Preparation

1 Read Tom's profile. Match 1–3 with paragraphs A–C.

1 personality ☐
2 hobbies and interests ☐
3 introduction, with personal information ☐

A I'm Tom and I'm 16 years old. I'm at Saint Mary's School. I'm in year 12. I live with my mum and dad and my two sisters.

B My hobbies are playing the guitar and going out with my friends. I'm also interested in fashion. I'm not very keen on sport, but I sometimes go ice-skating.

C I think I'm quite confident and my friends say I'm very ambitious. I get on well with funny people.

2 Underline phrases in Tom's profile with a similar meaning to the ones below.

1 I go to .... school
2 My name's …
3 I believe …
4 I like …
5 I'm quite a … person
6 I don't really like …

3 Put the lines of Mandy's profile in the correct order.

☐ Harry and I go to Hillcrest School.
☐ I live with my parents and older brother, Harry.
☐1 My name's Mandy.
☐ I'm 16 years old and I'm from Hastings.
☐ As for sport, I play hockey at school.
☐5 I've got lots of hobbies and interests.
☐ I also enjoy dancing.
☐ I like drawing and I spend a lot of time reading.
☐9 I'm quite talkative.
☐ I'm very lazy.
☐ I've probably got one big fault.
☐ In fact I really love chatting on the phone with my friends.

CHALLENGE!

Write four true sentences using the phrases in the box. Use nouns (people or things) or *-ing* forms.

> I'm not very keen on …   I really enjoy …
> I quite like …   I'm very interested in …

I'm not very keen on computer games.
I really enjoy spending time with my friends.

1 _____
_____

2 _____
_____

3 _____
_____

4 _____
_____

4 Put the words in the correct order to make sentences.

1 ambitious / am / I / not at all
_____

2 is / Kate / mean / a bit
_____

3 my / is / very / best / loyal / friend
_____

4 tolerant / person / Henry / a / quite / is
_____

5 Toby / slightly / shy / is
_____

6 impatient / my brother / quite / is
_____

Writing task

5 In your notebook write a personal profile of a friend or family member. Write 70–80 words and include this information:

- an introduction with your name, hometown, age, and brief information about your school and family.
- information about hobbies, interests and sports.
- a description of your personality.

Check your work

Have you
☐ included all the information?
☐ written 70–80 words?
☐ checked grammar, spelling and punctuation?

SELF CHECK 1

Read the clues and complete the crossword.

CLUES

Across (→)

2 The opposite of *patient*

7 He never tells the truth – he's very
   _____ .

8 I can't _____ laughing when my dad
   tries to dance.

10 'I love reading.'
   'Really? I can't _____ reading.'

13 He's very patient. He doesn't _____
   waiting if you're late.

15 Don't be _____! Share your sweets
   with your little brother.

16 'Is Pete sleeping?'
   'No, he _____.'

18 'I like playing chess.' '_____ too.'

19 Kate spends a lot of time _____
   TV.

20 My sister is very _____. She often
   tells jokes.

Down (↓)

1 'She doesn't say much.' 'No, she's very
   _____ .'

3 The opposite of *optimistic*

4 'I like playing computer games.'
   'Do you? What _____ do you like
   doing?'

5 I hope _____ study medicine at
   university next year.

6 '_____ you feel scared in lifts?' 'No,
   I don't.'

9 Sam _____ Patricia. He wants to
   marry her.

11 'Do they wear trainers to school?'
   'No, they _____ .'

12 You're very _____ – you should take
   more exercise.

14 I like watching football on TV, but I'd
   _____ play it.

17 The opposite of *hard-working*

Your score [   ] /20

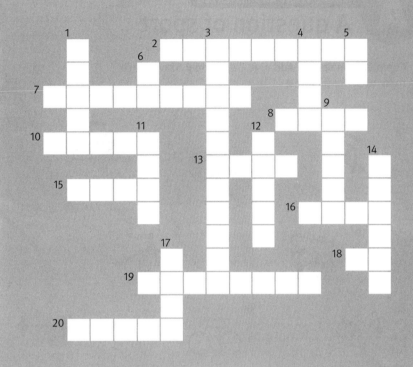

I CAN ...

Read the statements. Think about your progress and tick (✓) one of the
boxes.

✳ = I need more practice.   ✳✳ = I sometimes find this difficult.   ✳✳✳ = No problem!

	✳	✳✳	✳✳✳
I can describe someone's personality. (SB p.4)			
I can say what I usually do and what I'm doing now. (SB p.5)			
I can talk about hobbies and interests. (SB p.6)			
I can identify and use different verb patterns. (SB p.7)			
I can understand an article and a song about youth culture. (SB p.8)			
I can express my likes and dislikes. (SB p.10)			
I can write a personal profile for an Internet chatroom. (SB p.11)			

2 Winning and losing

A
VOCABULARY AND LISTENING
A question of sport

I can talk about sports I like.

1 Complete the sports. Add *a, e, i, o, u* and *y*. Then match them with the pictures.

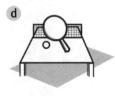

1 a t h l e t i c s   .....
2 b _ d m _ nt _ n .....
3 b _ s _ b _ ll   .....
4 b _ sk _ tb _ ll   .....
5 c _ cl _ ng   .....
6 f _ _ tb _ ll   .....
7 g _ lf   .....
8 g _ mn _ st _ cs .....
9 _ c _ h _ ck _ y .....
10 j _ d _   .....

11 k _ r _ t _   .....
12 r _ gb _   .....
13 s _ rf _ ng   .....
14 sw _ mm _ ng   .....
15 t _ bl _ t _ nn _ s .....
16 t _ nn _ s   .....
17 v _ lleyb _ ll   .....
18 w _ _ ght –
     l _ ft _ ng   .....

2 Write the sports from exercise 1 in the correct column.

play	do	go
_____	athletics	_____
_____	_____	_____
_____	_____	_____
_____	_____	_____
_____	_____	_____
_____	_____	_____
_____	_____	_____
_____	_____	_____
_____	_____	_____

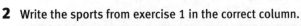

●●●●● **Extension:** Collocation: sports and games

3 Complete the sentences. Use the words in the box. Use the past simple form of the verbs.

| ~~compete~~   lose   miss   pass   score   win   serve |

1 Carl Lewis ___competed___ in four Olympic Games and _____ nine gold medals.
2 Fabio Grosso _____ the winning goal in the 2006 World Cup Final.
3 Maurice Baker _____ the ball to Darius Rice, who threw the ball into the basket.
4 Thierry Henry scored two goals, but France still _____ the match.
5 David Beckham _____ a penalty against Turkey in 2003. The match finished 0–0.
6 Venus Williams has the fastest serve in women's tennis. In 1998 she _____ the ball at 206 km / h.

Extra Practice

2B GRAMMAR
Past simple

I can describe past events.

1 Complete the text. Use the past simple of the verbs in brackets.

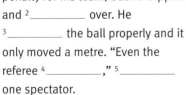

World Champion

Tanni Grey-Thompson is one of the most successful disabled athletes in the world. She ¹_____ (be) born with spina bifida, so she ²_____ (not can) walk and ³_____ (have to) use a wheelchair. At school her teachers ⁴_____ (not expect) her to be good at sport but her disability ⁵_____ (not stop) her and she ⁶_____ (swim) and ⁷_____ (play) basketball. Then she ⁸_____ (see) the London Marathon on TV and ⁹_____ (decide) to try athletics. At the age of 15 she ¹⁰_____ (represent) Wales in the Junior National Games and ¹¹_____ (come) first in the 100 metres. Between 1992 and 2004 she ¹²_____ (win) sixteen Paralympic medals and ¹³_____ (break) 30 world records. She ¹⁴_____ (retire) from wheelchair racing in 2007.

2 Complete the texts. Use the past simple of the verbs in the boxes.

Funny football stories

fall	not kick	laugh	say	~~try~~

In 1991, in a British cup final match, Peter Devine ¹ _tried_ to take a penalty for his team, but he tripped and ²_____ over. He ³_____ the ball properly and it only moved a metre. "Even the referee ⁴_____," ⁵_____ one spectator.

eat	not leave	~~play~~	show	want

In 1989, the Italian football team Pianta ⁶ _played_ a match against Arpax. The referee ⁷_____ to send off one of the Pianta players, D'Ercoli, so he ⁸_____ him the red card, but D'Ercoli ⁹_____ the pitch. He took the red card from the referee and ¹⁰_____ it!

3 Complete the sentences with the negative form of the verbs.

1 He won a silver medal, but he __didn't win__ a gold medal.
2 I was at the final of the World Cup in 2006 but I _____ at the final in 2002.
3 She competed in the Sydney Olympics but she _____ in the Athens Olympics.
4 My dad learned to ride a bike but he _____ to swim.
5 We played volleyball last night. We _____ basketball.
6 I was happy when Wayne Rooney scored a goal, but I _____ happy when the referee sent him off.
7 She saw the London Marathon, but she _____ the New York Marathon.

4 Write true sentences about what you did last weekend. Use the past simple, affirmative or negative, and the phrases in the box.

go to the cinema	have an argument with my parents
buy a CD	drink coffee at breakfast
meet my friends	read a book

1 I went / didn't go to the cinema.
2 _____
3 _____
4 _____
5 _____
6 _____

5 Put the words in the correct order to make questions. Then write true answers.

1 last / what / you / did / night / do / ?
What did you do last night?
_____

2 last / you / what / do / did / Sunday / ?
_____
_____

3 you / how many hours / last night / did / sleep / ?
_____
_____

4 do / on your last birthday / did / what / you / ?
_____
_____

5 did / last summer / where / go / you / on holiday / ?
_____
_____

Extra Practice

2C CULTURE
On the river

I can understand information about a sportsperson.

Revision: Student's Book page 16

1 Complete the sentences about the Oxford–Cambridge boat race. Use the words in the box.

> annual   cox   dead heat   record   rowers
> spectators   ~~takes place~~   take part   teams

1 The boat race __takes place__ in London.
2 It is an _____ event.
3 There are two _____ (one from Oxford and one from Cambridge).
4 In each boat there are eight _____ and a _____, who steers.
5 Lots of _____ watch the race from the banks of the river.
6 In 1877 both boats finished at exactly the same time – it was a _____ .
7 In 1982 Sue Brown was the first woman to _____ in the race.
8 In 1998 Cambridge set a new _____ for the course – 16 minutes and 19 seconds.

2 Read the text. How many Olympic gold medals did Steve Redgrave win? Choose the correct answer.

a four   b five   c six

A great rower

September 23rd 2000 was a special day for British rower, Steve Redgrave. He was rowing in the final of the 'coxless four' (four rowers without a cox) at the Olympic Games in Sydney, Australia. The spectators on the bank were cheering as the boat finished the race.

He and his team won the race by 0.3 seconds, with the Italian team second and the Australian team third.

It was Redgrave's fifth Olympic gold medal. He also won gold medals in Los Angeles (1984), Seoul (1988), Barcelona (1992) and Atlanta (1996), and a bronze medal in Seoul. It was an incredible achievement. Only four other sportspeople have won gold medals in five different Olympic Games. Redgrave has also won nine World Championship gold medals, and he holds one world record and one Olympic record. But he doesn't just row. He also likes winter sports and in 1998 was a member of the British bobsleigh team.

3 Choose the correct answer.

1 In a 'coxless four' there are
  A three rowers and a cox ☐   B four rowers and no cox ☐

2 Redgrave and his team won the final
  A by less than a second ☐   B by more than a second ☐

3 Redgrave won his first gold medal in
  A Los Angeles ☐   B Sydney ☐

4 Redgrave also won an Olympic
  A silver medal ☐   B bronze medal ☐

5 Redgrave holds
  A two records ☐   B nine records ☐

6 Redgrave also likes
  A winter sports ☐   B water sports ☐

●●●●● CHALLENGE! ●●●●●

Write a short text (about 30 words) about a sportsperson you like. Include this information:
- name and nationality
- his/her sport
- his/her biggest achievement / success
- why you like him/her

A sportsperson I really like is _____
_____
_____
_____
_____
_____

Steve Redgrave rowing in Sydney

2D GRAMMAR
Past simple and continuous

I can tell a short story using past tenses.

1 Choose the correct tense: past simple or past continuous.

Last winter, I ¹**had / was having** a nasty accident while I ²**skied / was skiing**. I was with my friend Joe. It was a beautiful morning. The sun ³**shone / was shining** and lots of people ⁴**skied / were skiing**. Suddenly, Joe ⁵**lost / was losing** control as he was going round a corner and ⁶**crashed / was crashing** into me. I ⁷**fell / was falling** and broke my leg. An air ambulance ⁸**arrived / was arriving** and ⁹**took / was taking** me to hospital. I was in hospital for two weeks!

●●●●● CHALLENGE! ●●●●●

Complete the sentences. Use *did, didn't, was, wasn't, were* or *weren't*.

1 '_Were_ you playing volleyball when he arrived?' 'No, we _____.'
2 '_____ she win the race?' 'Yes, she _____.'
3 '_____ you watch the match while you _____ having dinner?' 'No, we _____.'
4 What _____ you do when you got home?
5 '_____ he ring while she _____ doing her homework?' 'Yes, he _____.'
6 'How many goals _____ he score?' 'He _____ score any goals. He _____ playing!'

2 Complete the sentences. Use the past simple or past continuous of the verbs in brackets.

Last year my dad and I ¹_____visited_____ (visit) the USA. While we ²_____ (stay) in Los Angeles, we ³_____ (go) to a basketball game between the Los Angeles Lakers and the Chicago Bulls. The atmosphere inside the stadium ⁴_____ (be) really exciting. Thousands of spectators ⁵_____ (cheer). The Los Angeles Lakers ⁶_____ (score) 30 points in the last 10 minutes, but they ⁷_____ (not win). After the game, one of the players ⁸_____ (throw) the ball into the crowd and a man in front of us ⁹_____ (catch) it. While we ¹⁰_____ (leave) the stadium, the man ¹¹_____ (give) us the ball and ¹²_____ (say): 'Here's a souvenir!'

3 Look at the pictures and write the story. Use the prompts to help you.

Last month Joe and Sally / go / the motorbike Grand Prix. The sun / shine / and the crowd / be / happy. Joe and Sally / stand / near the finish line.

The race / be / really exciting. Two riders / race / very close. On the last corner / Colin Edwards / lead. Suddenly, / Nicky Hayden / pass / Edwards. Edwards / be / surprised. He / lose / control of his motorbike.

Edwards / crash / 500m before the finish line. While he / check / his motorbike, eleven other riders / finish / the race. Hayden / win / the Grand Prix, but the crowd / cheer / when Edwards / cross / the finish line!

Revision: Student's Book page 18

1 Label the picture with the words in the box.

beach   island   shark   surfer   surfboard   wave

2 Complete the article with the words in the box.

attacking   clear   eventually   professional
screamed   swimming   thought

3 Answer the questions.

1 Where were the swimmers?
_____

2 How many dolphins appeared?
_____

3 Why were the swimmers worried at first?
_____

4 What did one of the swimmers try to do?
_____

5 Why did one of the swimmers scream?
_____

6 How long did the dolphins stay with the swimmers?
_____

4 Put the events of the story in the correct order.

☐ One of the swimmers screamed when she saw a shark.
☐ The dolphins started to swim around the people.
☐ Ron tried to swim back to the beach.
☐ 1 The lifeguards were on a training swim.
☐ The shark swam away.
☐ Ten dolphins appeared.
☐ The dolphins stayed with the swimmers for 40 minutes.
☐ The shark tried to attack the swimmers.
☐ The swimmers returned to the beach.
☐ The dolphins pushed Ron back to other swimmers.

Friendly dolphins save swimmers

One morning in November 2004, four people were
¹_____ in the sea about 100 metres from the
beach near Auckland, New Zealand. They were
²_____ lifeguards on a training swim. Suddenly,
about ten dolphins appeared and started to swim around
them in circles. At first the swimmers were worried – they
³_____ that the dolphins were ⁴_____
them. One of the swimmers, Ron Howes, tried to swim
back to the beach, but the dolphins stopped him and
pushed him back to other swimmers. Suddenly, one of
the swimmers ⁵_____. There was a three-metre

shark and it was swimming towards them through the
⁶_____ blue water. It came very close to the
swimmers. It was only metres away, but it couldn't
attack them because the dolphins were there. The
dolphins stayed with the swimmers for 40 minutes.
⁷_____ the shark swam away and the dolphins
let the swimmers return to the beach. A scientist,
Rosemary Finn, who studies the behaviour of dolphins
wasn't surprised when she heard the story. 'Dolphins
often help other animals and fish when they are in
trouble in the sea,' she said.

2F EVERYDAY ENGLISH
Talking about the past

I can chat about what happened at the weekend.

1 Complete the labels with the verbs in the box.

| chat | go | go | go | ~~have~~ | help | take | tidy | visit |

1 ___have___ friends to stay

2 _____ with my friends on the phone

3 _____ my parents with the housework

4 _____ out with friends

5 _____ the dog for a walk

6 _____ my relatives

7 _____ my bedroom

8 _____ shopping

9 _____ away for the weekend

2 Choose the best reply.

1 I had a terrible weekend.
   A Oh dear. ☐
   B It was OK. ☐
2 What did you do on Friday evening?
   A I didn't. ☐
   B Nothing much. ☐
3 Did you have a good weekend?
   A It was OK. ☐
   B We're having relatives to stay. ☐
4 I went to the cinema.
   A Cool. What did you see? ☐
   B Oh dear. ☐

3 Match the follow-up questions in the box with the sentences. Then write answers.

Cool. Where did you go?   Really? Who did you visit?
Did you win?   What film did you see?
~~Really? What did you buy?~~

1 I went shopping.
   Really? What did you buy?   A CD and a DVD.
2 I went to the cinema.
   _____
3 I went out with some friends.
   _____
4 We visited some relatives.
   _____
5 I played in a volleyball match.
   _____

4 Complete the conversation with the questions in the box.

What did you watch?   What did you do on Sunday?
Did you have a good   What did you do on Saturday?
weekend?   What did you read?

Chris 1 _____
Peter Yes, I did.
Chris 2 _____
Peter I read a book.
Chris 3 _____
Peter A detective story.
Chris 4 _____
Peter I stayed in and watched TV.
Chris 5 _____
Peter A volleyball match and a film.

5 Write a conversation like the one in exercise 4, with five questions and five replies. Use activities from exercise 1.

A Did you _____ ?
B Yes, _____
A What _____ Saturday ?
B _____
A _____ ?
B _____
A What _____ Sunday?
B _____
A _____ ?
B _____

Extra Practice

Unit 2 • Winning and losing   17

A magazine article

I can write an article for a student magazine.

Preparation

1 Complete the text with the words in the box.

admire   coach   famous   joined   matches   played
retired   scored   team   win

2 Match the headings (1–4) with the paragraphs (A–D).

1 Early successes ☐
2 Why I admire him ☐
3 Family and early years ☐
4 Later years ☐

Ferenc Puskás

A Ferenc Puskás was a ¹_____ Hungarian footballer. He was born in 1927 in Budapest. His father was a football ²_____, so Ferenc started playing at an early age.

B At the age of 16 Puskás joined Honved football club and helped them to ³_____ five Hungarian league titles. In 1945 he ⁴_____ for Hungary for the first time, and was a member of the ⁵_____ that won the Olympic Gold medal in 1952.

C In 1956 he left Hungary, and in 1958 he ⁶_____ Real Madrid. Although he was already in his thirties, he won the Spanish league five times and the European Cup three times before he ⁷_____ in 1967, at the age of forty.

D I ⁸_____ him because he ⁹_____ in almost every match he played in – 357 goals in 354 ¹⁰_____ for Honved, 154 goals in 179 matches for Real Madrid and 83 goals in 84 matches for Hungary!

Writing task

3 In your notebook write an article (130–150) words about a sportsperson or another famous person. Divide your article into three or four paragraphs. Choose one of these topics for each paragraph:

- Family and early years
- Early successes
- Later years
- Greatest achievements
- Why you admire him/her

Check your work

Have you

☐ divided your article into paragraphs, each with its own topic?
☐ written 130–150 words?
☐ checked grammar, spelling and punctuation?

CHALLENGE!

Match the people with their achievements.

1 _____ won the Tour de France cycle race seven times in succession.

2 _____ won 18 singles titles, 31 women's doubles titles and 10 mixed doubles titles.

3 _____ won gold medals at four successive Paralympics (from 1992 to 2004).

4 _____ won the World Heavyweight Boxing Championship three times.

5 _____ was the first gymnast to receive a perfect score of 10.0 at the Olympics.

6 _____ is a retired American athlete who won five Olympic gold medals.

7 _____ is the only footballer ever to win three World Cups.

8 _____ was four times World Figure Skating champion.

a Katarina Witt

b Tanni Grey-Thompson

c Nadia Komaneci

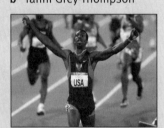
d Michael Johnson

e Lance Armstrong

f Pele

g Martina Navratilova

h Muhammad Ali

Extra Practice

SELF CHECK 2

Read the clues and complete the crossword.

CLUES

Across (→)

1 It _____ raining. It was hot and sunny.

6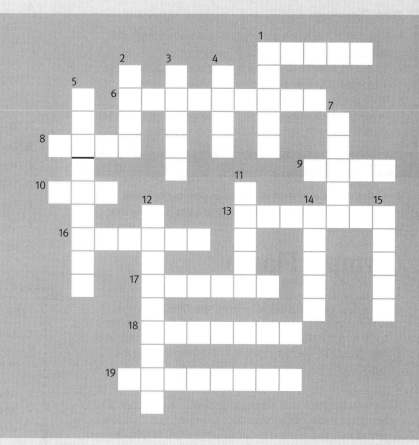

8 We _____ playing rugby when it started to rain.

9 *rang* is the past simple form of _____ .

10 The past simple form of *win* is _____ .

13 The past simple form of *cheat* is _____ .

16

17 Rooney _____ a penalty in the last minute, so England lost the match.

18 'What are you doing this evening?' '_____ much.'

19 John _____ in three races in an athletics competition.

Down (↓)

1 He arrived _____ we were having lunch.

2 My brother _____ me a CD for my birthday.

3 '_____ did you go?' 'To the park.'

4 Last weekend I _____ surfing.

5

7 Federer only lost one _____ in that game.

11 'Did you _____ a goal?' 'Yes, it was the only goal in the match.'

12

14 'Did you have a good weekend?' 'Yes, I did. What _____ you?'

15 'Did Sarah's team win the volleyball match?' 'No, they _____ .'

Your score ___ /20

I CAN ...

Read the statements. Think about your progress and tick (✓) one of the boxes.

✱ = I need more practice.   ✱✱ = I sometimes find this difficult.   ✱✱✱ = No problem!

	✱	✱✱	✱✱✱
I can talk about sports I like. (SB p.14)			
I can describe past events. (SB p.15)			
I can understand information about a sporting event. (SB p.16)			
I can tell a short story using past tenses. (SB p.17)			
I can understand a magazine article. (SB p.18)			
I can chat about what happened at the weekend. (SB p.20)			
I can write an article for a student magazine. (SB p.21)			

Self Check • 2   **19**

• • • • • • • • • • • •

TIPS: Reading

- Read the paragraphs quickly to find out what the text is about.
- You don't need to understand every word to do the task. Try to guess the meaning of new words from context.
- Read the text again more carefully and match the headings to the paragraphs. Don't forget that there is one extra heading.

EXAM TASK – Reading

Read the article and choose the most suitable heading (A–G) for each paragraph. There is one extra heading that you do not need.

Olympic Flame

1 _____

Every four years the world watches the Olympic Games, which start when somebody from the host country carries a torch into the stadium and lights the flame in the opening ceremony. The flame continues to burn throughout the games until it is extinguished in the closing ceremony.

2 _____

This is a tradition that started in ancient Greece, when a fire burnt throughout the ancient Olympics, but it wasn't introduced to the modern games until 1928. The modern world welcomed the idea of an Olympic flame with enthusiasm. In 1936 Carl Diem, a German sports official, came up with the idea of an Olympic torch relay for the 1936 Summer Olympics in Berlin. Since then the torch relay has been part of the Olympic Games.

3 _____

The Olympic torch is lit many months before the opening ceremony at Olympia, the site of the ancient Olympics in Greece. Eleven women take part and one of them lights the torch from the sun using a special mirror. After this there is a ceremony in the Athenian Panathinaiko Stadium where the Athens city authorities deliver the torch to the officials of the host city.

4 _____

This ceremony is then followed by the torch relay. Traditionally, runners, including athletes, celebrities and ordinary people carry the torch on a journey from Athens to the host city. The relay lasts for many months and goes through many countries. Sometimes the torch travels by boat, or by plane.

5 _____

The relay ends when the torch arrives at the Olympic stadium where the Games will take place. The final carrier of the torch is often kept secret until the last moment, and is usually a famous sportsman or woman. They run around the track and towards a huge cauldron, which is usually at the top of a staircase. They use the torch to light the Olympic flame.

6 _____

The torch relay represents the passing of Olympic traditions from one generation to the next. Originally the flame represented the 'endeavour for protection and struggle for victory'. Since it was introduced again in 1928, it has come to represent 'the light of spirit, knowledge, and life'.

A The end of the journey
B The history of the flame
C The beginning of the Olympics
D The symbolic meaning of the flame
E The end of the Olympics
F Carrying the torch
G Lighting the torch

• • • • • • • • • • • • • • • • • •

TIPS: Use of English

- Read the whole text quickly to find out what it is about.
- You need to fill in the gaps with words like prepositions, modal verbs, auxiliary verbs, linkers, articles, relative pronouns, etc.
- You can write only ONE word in each gap.
- When you have finished, read the text again to check your answers.

EXAM TASK – Use of English

Read the anecdote about Pablo Picasso. Write the missing words (1–8). Use only one word in each gap.

There are many anecdotes about Pablo Picasso, the famous Spanish artist and sculptor. According [1]_____ his mother, Picasso learned to draw before he [2]_____ speak and his first word was 'pencil'. He was not a very good pupil and he [3]_____ to leave school because he could not remember the letters of the alphabet. When he became a world-famous artist, he [4]_____ often visited by other celebrities. Once Charlie Chaplin [5]_____ to see him in his studio. While Picasso was working [6]_____ one of his paintings, he accidentally spilt [7]_____ paint on Chaplin's trousers. Picasso immediately offered to get some alcohol to remove it but Chaplin said, 'Please, [8]_____. Just leave the paint where it is, and make sure you also sign my trousers.'

PREPARATION: Listening

1 Read the instructions and the notes below. Try to predict what you will hear in the recording. Answer the following questions:
   - How many places are listed in the notes?
   - What types of places are mentioned and what can you do there?

2 Try to guess what kind of vocabulary you might hear in the recordings.

EXAM TASK – Listening

🎧 LISTENING 1   Listen to the information about places to visit. Complete the notes.

LAKESIDE LEISURE CENTRE
- in Bracknell
- you can relax, get fit and have a tasty meal in a brand new ¹_____ restaurant

Facilities
- ²_____ swimming pools
- indoor and outdoor tennis courts
- a fitness room

Opening hours
- every day from ³_____ a.m. to ⁴_____ p.m. except on Sunday

QUEEN'S SQUARE SHOPPING CENTRE
- in Crawley
- all shops under one roof
- parking for ⁵_____ cars

BANBURY SAFARI PARK
- they have ⁶_____ species of animals

Opening hours
- all day
- from ⁷_____ o'clock in the morning to ⁸_____ at night
- entrance fee £⁹_____ for adults; £¹⁰_____ for children
- children under seven: ¹¹_____ charge

TIPS: Writing a magazine article

- Read the instructions and the questions carefully before you start to write.
- Brainstorm ideas for each question in the task and make notes.
- Organise your notes to form a writing plan. Use a mind map if this helps you.
- Write clear paragraphs for each point to want to make. Remember to give your own opinion.

EXAM TASK – Writing

The editors of an international student magazine have asked you to write an article (120–180 words) about young people and sport. They would like you to include the following points:

- What experience does the average teenage have of sport in your country?
- Do you think it's important for teenagers to play sport?
- How do famous sportspeople affect teenagers' lives?

TIPS: Speaking

- If you have to answer general questions about yourself in the speaking exam, don't give just one- or two-word answers. Give details and examples wherever possible.
- Try to use the correct tenses when answering the questions, e.g. the present simple to talk about habits and routines, the past simple to talk about your last holiday, etc.
- If you don't understand a question, ask the examiner to repeat it. Look at the Functions Bank on page 101 to find useful phrases.

EXAM TASK – Speaking

Work in pairs and ask each other the questions below. Your partner must have the book closed when you ask him/her the questions. Then change roles.

Questions

1 What do you most enjoy doing when you are at home?
2 Describe your best friend.
3 How do you spend your free time?
4 What's the most exciting thing you have ever done?
5 What would be an ideal career for you?
6 Where's the best place to spend a free afternoon around here?
7 Where did you spend your last holiday?
8 Do you think computers will replace newspapers and TV in the future?

3 Town and country

Landscapes

I can describe a place in the town or country.

1 Look at the pictures and complete the puzzle. Find the word that isn't illustrated (↓).

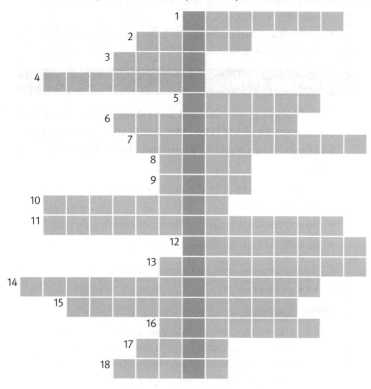

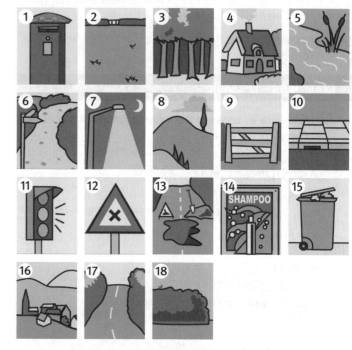

2 Complete the sentences with prepositions of movement, and match them to the pictures.

1 Mark walked _____ the postbox.
2 Sylvia ran _____ the pavement.
3 Jamie went _____ the bridge.
4 Beth rode _____ the fence.
5 Jessica drove _____ the gate.

●●●●● **Extension:** compound nouns

3 Complete the text using compound nouns: the noun in brackets plus a word from the box (before or after). Use a dictionary to check whether they are written as one word or two.

| basket | ~~centre~~ | computer | ends | pool | pop |
| sweat | table | work | | | |

Last Saturday I went shopping with my parents. We went to the new ¹ <u>shopping centre</u> (shopping) near our town. I bought a new ² _____ (shirt). My sister bought the new Britney Spears CD. I don't like ³ _____ (music) very much, so I hardly ever buy CDs.

In the afternoon I went to the sports centre with my friends Jake and Patricia. I always go there at ⁴ _____ (week). There's a really good ⁵ _____ (swimming) there, but we didn't go swimming. We played ⁶ _____ (tennis) and ⁷ _____ (ball). In the evening I did my ⁸ _____ (home), and then I played ⁹ _____ (games) with my sister.

Extra Practice

3B GRAMMAR
some, any, much, many, a lot, a few

I can talk about quantities.

1 Complete Penny's e-mail to her penfriend with *some* and *any*.

Hi Maria

I hope you're well. Sorry I haven't sent you ¹_____ e-mails recently. I had exams all last week! I think they went OK, but I haven't had ²_____ results yet. Have you got ³_____ exams this term?

I'm going shopping in New York tomorrow with ⁴_____ friends. We're going to the department stores to buy ⁵_____ new clothes. There aren't ⁶_____ department stores near my house. There are ⁷_____ good clothes shops in town, but they're expensive. Are there ⁸_____ good shops where you live?

Write soon
Love
Penny

2 Look at the picture. Choose the correct expression to complete the sentences.

1 There is **a lot of** / **a little** traffic.
2 There aren't **many** / **any** fields.
3 There are **a lot of** / **a few** street lights.
4 There aren't **many** / **any** pedestrians.
5 There are **a few** / **a lot of** advertisements.
6 There aren't **a few** / **any** hedges.

3 Which endings for these sentences are correct? Tick (✓) A, B or both.

1 In this village, you don't see many
   A cars. ☐   B traffic. ☐
2 On the High Street, you can find a few
   A rubbish. ☐   B shops. ☐
3 Our house is in the middle of a lot of beautiful
   A fields. ☐   B scenery. ☐
4 The village doesn't have much
   A pollution. ☐   B street lamps. ☐
5 The petrol station sells a few
   A food. ☐   B books. ☐
6 Can you see any
   A water? ☐   B roadworks? ☐

4 Complete the description of New York. Choose the best words.

I♥NY

New York is one the most exciting cities in the world. There are ¹**lots of** / **much** things to do in Manhattan, the heart of New York. There are hundreds of museums, restaurants, cafés, clubs and theatres to visit, and ²**a little** / **a lot of** exclusive and expensive shops.

In the past the air was very polluted, but now there isn't ³**some** / **much** pollution. In fact, New York is now a very clean city. There's ⁴**much** / **a lot of** beautiful scenery around the city. On Long Island, only ⁵**a few** / **many** miles from New York, you can find ⁶**some** / **any** fantastic beaches, and to the west of the city even ⁷**much** / **a few** mountains where you can ski.

New Yorkers are very welcoming – you won't find ⁸**much** / **many** unfriendly people. So come and spend ⁹**a little** / **a few** time in New York. You won't regret it!

● ● ● ● ● ● **CHALLENGE!** ● ● ● ● ● ●

Write five sentences describing the place where you live. Use the words in the box to help you.

block of flats	car	factory	farm	fresh air	noise
busy road	hill	lane	night-life	pollution	scenery
traffic	wood

There aren't many factories in my town.
There's some beautiful scenery around my village.

1 _____
2 _____
3 _____
4 _____
5 _____

3C CULTURE The United Kingdom

I can understand information in a guidebook.

Revision: Student's Book page 26

1 Complete the sentences about Wales with the words in the box.

> Celtic   farming   independent   industrial
> kayaking   population   situated   spectacular

1 Wales is not _____. It's part of the UK.
2 Most of the _____ of Wales live in the south.
3 In the north, there are _____ lakes, valleys and rivers.
4 The most _____ part of the country is the south.
5 Cardiff is _____ in the south.
6 Welsh is a _____ language.
7 People come to Wales to go _____ on the rivers.
8 _____ is an important industry in Wales.

2 Read the text about Scotland. Match paragraphs 1–4 with the missing first sentences. There is one extra sentence that you don't need to use.

a The scenery in Scotland is spectacular.
b Many famous people come from Scotland.
c Tourism is an important industry in Scotland.
d Scotland isn't an independent state.
e People in Scotland speak English.

SCOTLAND

1 ☐ It is part of the UK. It is situated in the north of Britain. It has a population of about five million and the capital is Edinburgh. Most of the population live in the south of the country.

2 ☐ The north of Scotland is called the Highlands because there are a lot of mountains, including Ben Nevis, the highest mountain in the UK. There are also beautiful lakes and woods.

3 ☐ There is also a Scottish language called Gaelic, which is a Celtic language. However, only about 60,000 people in Scotland now speak it. Most of them live in the Highlands.

4 ☐ Edinburgh and Glasgow are two exciting cities in the south. Many people visit the north of Scotland to enjoy the clean air and wonderful scenery. One of the most famous tourist attractions in this region is Loch Ness, home of the Loch Ness monster!

3 Complete the fact file about Scotland.

Location	in the north of Britain
Population	
Capital	
Highest mountain	
Languages	and
Important industry	
Famous tourist attraction	

4 Read the sentences. Are they true or false for the place where you live? Write T or F.

1 There aren't many people here. ____
2 There's a lot of beautiful scenery. ____
3 There's a lot for young people to do. ____
4 There's a lot of pollution. ____
5 The people are very friendly. ____
6 It's an exciting place to live. ____
7 It's a very industrial region. ____
8 It's difficult to find jobs here. ____

5 Write two advantages and two disadvantages of living where you live. Use ideas from exercise 4 or your own ideas.

Advantages: _____

_____

Disadvantages: _____

_____

●●●●● **CHALLENGE!** ●●●●●

Do the quiz about Wales. Then check your answers with a partner.

1 What is the population of Wales?
  A 3 million   B 13 million   C 30 million
2 How much of the population speaks Welsh?
  A 100%   B 75%   C 20%
3 What is the capital of Wales?
  A Dublin   B Edinburgh   C Cardiff
4 Which of these cities is in Wales?
  A Swansea   B Liverpool   C Manchester
5 What is the name of the highest mountain in Wales?
  A Snowdon   B Everest   C Fuji
6 Which of these famous actresses is Welsh?
  A Angelina Jolie
  B Catherine Zeta-Jones
  C Penélope Cruz

24   Unit 3 • Town and country

3D GRAMMAR Articles

I can correctly use 'a / an' and 'the' with nouns.

1 Complete the sentences. Use *a* or *an* and the words in the box. Then add three more similar sentences about famous people in your country.

actor actress artist composer footballer
politician singer

1 Beethoven was _____.
2 Pelé was _____.
3 Tony Blair is _____.
4 Johnny Depp is _____.
5 Elton John is _____.
6 Pablo Picasso was _____.
7 Catherine Zeta-Jones is _____.
8 _____.
9 _____.
10 _____.

2 Complete the sentences with *a* or *an* in one gap and *the* in the other.

1 He lives in _____ small town in _____ north of Scotland.
2 She's _____ computer programmer in _____ army.
3 He's _____ only person in the photo who's wearing _____ hat.
4 She's _____ journalist with _____ New York Times.
5 I always watch _____ DVD at _____ weekend.
6 _____ head teacher at my school has got _____ new car.
7 My sister is _____ lead singer of _____ rock group.
8 _____ teacher at my school lives by _____ sea.

3 Which sentences need a definite article (*the*) and which are generalizations? Tick (✓) or complete.

1 I don't like _____ Mondays. ✓
2 I'll see you at __the__ weekend.
3 I don't really like _____ heavy metal music.
4 I really like _____ new Black Eyed Peas CD.
5 I never wear _____ jeans.
6 _____ tigers live in Asia.
7 Polar bears don't mind _____ cold weather.
8 I'm not enjoying _____ cold weather this winter.
9 He's reading _____ new Harry Potter book.
10 I don't read _____ books about magic.

4 Read the *Look out!* box and look at the countries below. Write *The* or tick (✓) if no article is needed.

> **Look out!**
>
> We don't use *The* with the names of countries, unless the country's title includes a word like: republic, kingdom, state

1 __The__ United Kingdom
2 _____ Great Britain
3 _____ Republic of Ireland
4 _____ South Africa
5 _____ United States
6 _____ Czech Republic

5 Complete the text with *a/an* or *the*.

We recently moved to South Milton, which is ¹__a__ small village near the sea. My dad's ²_____ doctor, and he got ³_____ new job here. At first, I thought it was ⁴_____ most boring place in ⁵_____ whole world, because ⁶_____ nearest town is 15 kilometres away. But I have new hobbies now.

I love going to the beach and going out to sea in my kayak, which is ⁷_____ small boat. I go every day when ⁸_____ weather is good, and even when it's bad!

I also have ⁹_____ job in ¹⁰_____ village post office to earn some money. I really like my life in ¹¹_____ countryside now.

> ●●●●●● **CHALLENGE!** ●●●●●●
>
> Complete the advertisement. Write *a*, *an*, *the* or a tick (✓) if no article is needed.
>
> Is ¹ __✓__ fun important for you? Do you enjoy ² ___ excitement of ³ ___ big cities? Or are you looking for ⁴ ___ relaxing break? Whatever you need, we have the perfect holiday for you. Spend ⁵ ___ few days in North Wales – ⁶ ___ scenery is amazing and there are lots of lakes and rivers for people who like ⁷ ___ water sports. Or how about ⁸ ___ weekend in New York? Spend the evening in a jazz club, and then climb ⁹ ___ Empire State Building for great views of ¹⁰ ___ city at night.

Revision: Student's Book page 28

1 Match the two halves of the sentences.

1 The house was **empty** – ☐
2 It's an **enormous** city – ☐
3 She's an **extraordinary** woman – ☐
4 He isn't **lonely** – ☐
5 It's a **rural** village – ☐
6 The roads are **silent** – ☐
7 It's a **tiny** farm – ☐

a she can speak eight languages.
b the population is about 8 million.
c there are fields all around it.
d there are only a few sheep.
e there aren't any cars.
f nobody was at home.
g he's got lots of friends.

2 Choose the correct word in these sentences.

1 It's a **stressful / relaxing** place to live. Everybody is busy all the time.
2 The town centre is **modern / old** – it was built less than thirty years ago.
3 It's a very **dangerous / safe** place to live. There isn't much crime.
4 The air in the city is very **clean / polluted** because of all the cars.
5 It's a very **boring / exciting** city – there's a lot to see and do.
6 A lot of tourists visit the lake because it's very **pretty / ugly**.
7 The village is quite **noisy / quiet** because it's very near a big airport.

3 Read the first sentence of each paragraph and match each paragraph with the correct topic.

Leaving St Kilda	☐	St Kilda today	☐
St Kilda around 1800	☐	Where is St Kilda?	☐

The Edge of the World

a It isn't an easy place to get to. It's in the Atlantic Ocean about 65 km west of the Outer Hebrides islands, which are to the north-west of Scotland. It takes 14 hours to get there from Scotland by boat. A few people visit the tiny islands of St Kilda every year, but not many.

4 Read the text and check your answers to exercise 3.

5 Are the sentences true or false? Correct the false sentences.

1 St Kilda is 65 km west of Scotland. ____

_____

2 It takes 14 hours to get from Scotland to St Kilda by boat. ____

_____

3 Not many people visit St Kilda. ____

4 Many inhabitants of St Kilda moved to other countries to find work. ____

_____

5 In 1930, the final 36 inhabitants wanted to stay on St Kilda. ____

_____

6 On 29 August 1930, the final 36 inhabitants went to Australia. ____

_____

7 There are only scientists on the islands today. ____

_____

8 There isn't any entertainment on the islands. ____

_____

b About two hundred years ago, the population of St Kilda was about 200. They had their own way of life. They climbed up the cliffs and caught sea birds for food. They had meetings in the village streets and made their own laws. They didn't have much contact with people from other places.

c But life was hard for the people of St Kilda, and many decided to leave the islands and travel to the USA or Australia to look for work. They wanted to earn money and have a better life. By 1930, there were only 36 inhabitants left. They decided that they wanted to leave too, and on 29 August, a boat arrived and took them to Scotland. They never returned.

d Today, there aren't any permanent inhabitants of St Kilda on the islands. However, the islands are not empty. Scientists live and work there, studying the sea birds and other wildlife. There are also a few soldiers. There isn't much entertainment, but at least there is now a sauna and a bar!

1 Look at the map. Complete the sentences with the prepositions of place in the box.

behind   between   near   next to
on the corner of   opposite

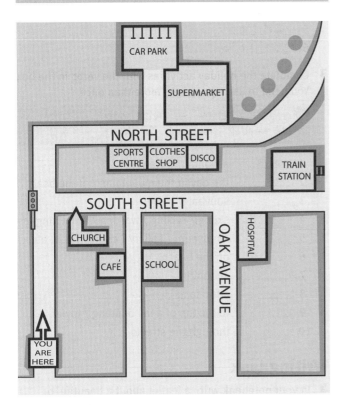

1 The clothes shop is _____ the sports centre and the disco.
2 The hospital is _____ South Street and Oak Avenue.
3 The school is _____ the café.
4 The car park is _____ the supermarket.
5 The disco is _____ the clothes shop.
6 The train station is _____ the hospital.

2 Write the words in the correct order to make directions.

1 straight / on / go

_____

2 end / to / go / the / the / road / of

_____

3 first / take / the / right

_____

4 traffic / turn / lights / the / at / right

_____

5 go / past / church / the

_____

6 North / along / Street / go

_____

3 Look at the map again. Use expressions from exercises 1 and 2 to complete these directions.

You   Excuse me. Is there a supermarket near here?
Man   Yes, there's one in North Street.
You   Can you tell me how to get there?
Man   Yes. [1] _____ and turn right.
          [2] _____ and the supermarket is on the left, [3] _____ the sports centre.
You   Thanks.

You   Excuse me. Is there a café near here?
Man   Yes, there is.
You   Can you tell me how to get there?
Man   Yes. [4] _____ traffic lights. [5] _____ the church and [6] _____ . The café is on the right, [7] _____ the school.
You   Thank you.

4 Choose two places from the box. Write similar dialogues giving directions.

clothes shop   disco   car park   train station

You   Excuse me. Is there _____
            _____ here?
Woman   Yes, there's one _____ .
You   Can you tell me _____ ?
Woman   Yes. _____
            _____
            _____
You   Thanks.

You   Excuse ____ . Is _____ ?
Man   Yes, _____
You   Can you _____
            _____ ?
Man   _____
            _____
            _____
You   _____

3G WRITING
A leaflet

I can write a leaflet describing places of interest.

Preparation

1 Complete the leaflets with the phrases in the box.

> **a** the beautiful sandy beaches
> **b** wonderful parks
> **c** the stunning views
> **d** the Ashmolean Museum and the Museum of Modern Art
> **e** the historic colleges
> **f** climbing, walking, kayaking

Historic Oxford

- Wander through the streets and visit ¹_____ _____ of the university.
- Take a boat trip on the beautiful River Thames and enjoy the beautiful scenery.
- Don't miss the beautiful paintings at ²_____ _____.
- Climb the 127 steps to the top of the tower of St Mary's Church and enjoy stunning views of the ancient city.
- Relax in one of Oxford's ³_____.

Come to Snowdonia in the Heart of Wales

- If you like outdoor activities, Snowdonia is the place for you. You can go ⁴_____ and lots more.
- Don't forget to visit the seaside. Wander along ⁵_____ or take a walk along the cliffs.
- Visit the historic town of Caernarfon, with its historic castle.
- Climb to the top of Snowdon, Britain's second-highest mountain, and enjoy ⁶_____ _____.

2 Complete the adjectives. Use *a, e, i, o* and *u*.

1 h_st_r_c
2 w_nd_rf_l
3 b___t_f_l
4 st_nn_ng
5 _nc__nt
6 f_nt_st_c

3 Complete the holiday activities with the verbs in the box. You need to use some verbs more than once.

> buy   climb   ~~enjoy~~   go   relax   spend   take
> visit   wander

1 __enjoy__ a wonderful view
2 _____ the day in the mountains / at the beach
3 _____ souvenirs
4 _____ skiing / cycling / walking / swimming, etc.
5 _____ a museum / gallery / church / zoo, etc.
6 _____ on the beach
7 _____ shopping
8 _____ a trip to ...
9 _____ to the top of a tall building / tower
10 _____ through the streets

Writing task

4 In your notebook write a leaflet about a beautiful or interesting place in your country. Use the Writing Bank on page 103 to help you. Write 70–80 words and include this information:

- a title to attract attention.
- information about interesting places to see and visit.
- information about what people can do there.

Check your work

Have you
- [ ] used bullet points?
- [ ] used a variety of adjectives to make your descriptions interesting?
- [ ] written 70–80 words?
- [ ] checked grammar, spelling and punctuation?

Extra Practice

SELF CHECK 3

Read the clues and complete the crossword.

CLUES

Across (→)

4 The bus got stuck in a _____ so we were late for school.

7 The bank is _____ the cinema and the post office.

8 We live by _____ sea.

9 There are two clothes shops in the shopping _____ .

12 My uncle is _____ actor.

14 There isn't _____ pollution in our village.

15 Turn left and go _____ the church. The shop is on the left.

17 There are _____ fields near our school.

19 I've got a black jacket and a brown jacket. I like _____ black jacket best.

Down (↓)

1 It's very dark. They should turn on the _____ .

2 Close the _____ when you leave the garden.

3 About 200 people live in my _____ .

5 Hurry up! The train goes in _____ minutes.

6 _____ weather wasn't very good yesterday.

9 We waited for the taxi on the _____ of Green Street and Newtown Road.

10 There's a rubbish bin _____ to the post box.

11 _____ me. Is there a library near here?

13 The dog ran _____ the gate into the road.

16 Are there _____ shops in your village?

18 Go straight _____ and turn right at the traffic lights.

Your score [   ] /20

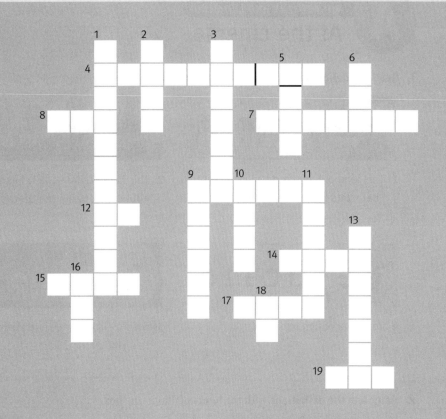

I CAN ...

Read the statements. Think about your progress and tick (✓) one of the boxes.

✱ = I need more practice.   ✱✱ = I sometimes find this difficult.   ✱✱✱ = No problem!

	✱	✱✱	✱✱✱
I can describe a place in the town or country. (SB p.24)			
I can talk about quantities. (SB p.25)			
I can understand information in a guidebook. (SB p.26)			
I can correctly use 'a/an' and 'the' with nouns. (SB p.27)			
I can understand a newspaper article. (SB p.28)			
I can understand and give directions. (SB p.30)			
I can write a leaflet describing places of interest. (SB p.31)			

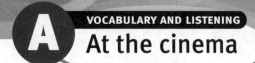

4 In the spotlight

A VOCABULARY AND LISTENING
At the cinema

I can talk about different types of film.

1 Read the definitions and write the types of film.

1 This kind of film often includes scary characters like vampires and zombies.
horror film

2 This kind of film usually has a story about cowboys in the USA.

3 This kind of film includes songs and dancing.

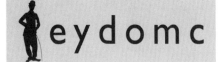

4 This kind of film makes you laugh.

5 Studios like Disney and Pixar make this kind of film.

6 This kind of film is about a large and terrible event, like a tsunami, an earthquake or a huge fire.

2 Complete the definitions with the types of film in the box.

action films   historical dramas   romantic comedies
science fiction films   war films

1 _____ show a specific period in the past. You can see how people dressed, spoke and behaved in those days.
2 _____ are films about soldiers and battles.
3 _____ often show the future. They sometimes include aliens.
4 _____ are love stories that are also funny.
5 _____ are fast, exciting films that often contain fights and car chases.

3 Choose the correct word.

1 The film was really **gripping / moving**. It made me cry!
2 I don't like war films. They're too **funny / violent**.
3 I couldn't watch the end of the horror film – it was too **entertaining / scary**.
4 The special effects were OK but the story was really **boring / gripping**. I fell asleep!
5 I enjoyed the musical – the songs and dancing were really **entertaining / violent**.
6 The story is **funny / gripping** – you really want to know what is going to happen.
7 I laughed a lot – it's a really **funny / scary** film.

●●●●● **Extension: -ed and -ing adjectives**

4 Complete the sentences by adding -ed or -ing.

1 I was annoy _ed_ because I missed the beginning of the film.
2 This romantic comedy has a very surpris____ ending.
3 I'm not interest____ in war films. I think they're boring.
4 I sat next to the wrong person in the cinema. I was so embarrass____!
5 Most of the film wasn't very scary, but the ending was really frighten____.
6 It was a confus____ film – the plot was very difficult to understand.
7 I love action films because they're excit____.
8 The film was too long. I was bor____ by the end.
9 I loved the story. I was gripp____ from beginning to end.
10 I really liked the story, but I was disappoint____ by the acting.

Extra Practice

Comparatives and superlatives

I can make comparisons.

1 Write the missing forms of these adjectives.

scary	<u>scarier</u>	<u>the scariest</u>
mean	_____	_____
generous	_____	_____
_____	bigger	_____
small	_____	_____
hot	_____	_____
	_____	the coldest
good	_____	_____
_____	worse	_____
funny	_____	_____
_____	_____	the most serious
good-looking	_____	_____
_____		the ugliest

2 Write true sentences using the comparative form of the adjectives in brackets.

1 silver / gold (heavy)
<u>Gold is heavier than silver.</u>

2 Norway / Brazil (warm)
_____

3 April / January (short)
_____

4 fruit / junk food (healthy)
_____

5 Hungary / Poland (small)
_____

6 Fiats / Ferraris (expensive)
_____

7 tigers / horses (dangerous)
_____

3 Complete the sentences with your own ideas and the comparative form.

1 Kirsten Dunst is beautiful but <u>Halle Berry is more beautiful</u>.
2 *The Matrix* is gripping, but _____
_____.
3 Jim Carrey is funny, but _____
_____.
4 War films are exciting, but _____
_____.
5 *Big Momma's House 2* is a bad film, but _____
_____.
6 Mercedes cars are expensive, but _____
_____.
7 The England football team is good, but _____
_____.

4 Complete the questions with the superlative form of the adjectives. Then choose the correct answer.

1 Jupiter is (large) <u>the largest</u>   <u>d</u>
2 The Volga is (long) _____ ___
3 *Titanic* is (successful) _____ ___
4 The Caspian Sea is (big) _____ ___
5 London Heathrow is (busy) _____ ___
6 Djibouti in Africa is (hot) _____ ___

a river in Europe
b airport in the world.
c lake in the world.
d planet in the solar system.
e country in the world.
f disaster film of all time.

5 Complete the text with the comparative or superlative form of the adjectives in brackets.

Naomi Watts isn't one of the
¹ <u>the youngest</u> (young) actresses in
Hollywood – she was born in 1968
– but at the moment, she is one of
the ² _____ (popular). Some
actresses become famous almost
immediately, but for Naomi, it has
been a ³ _____ (long) and
⁴ _____ (difficult) process. Her ⁵ _____
(big) role so far is Ann Darrow in *King Kong*, one of the
⁶ _____ (successful) films of 2005. However, she
has been a film actress since 1986 and before *King Kong*,
appeared in many ⁷ _____ (small) films.

●●●●●● **CHALLENGE!** ●●●●●●

Complete the questions with the comparative or superlative form of the adjectives. Then answer the questions.

1 What is <u>the biggest</u> (big) country in the world?
_____

2 Is the Atlantic Ocean _____ (large) or
_____ (small) than the Pacific Ocean?
_____

3 Which is _____ (cold) continent in the world?
_____

4 Is gold _____ (heavy) than silver?
_____

5 What's _____ (high) mountain in the world?
_____

6 Which is _____ (near) to the sun: Mars or Earth?
_____

4C

CULTURE

Licensed to kill

I can talk about a famous film character.

Revision: Student's Book page 36

1 Complete the summary of the Student's Book text about James Bond. Use the words in the box.

> actors   agent   author   character   charming
> journalist   part   Service   thrillers   War

The British are not famous for action films, but the Bond films are very successful. The main ¹_____, James Bond, is an intelligence ²_____. He is reckless, but also ³_____ – especially with women. Bond first appeared in books by the British ⁴_____ Ian Fleming. Fleming was originally a ⁵_____ who worked for the British Intelligence ⁶_____ during the Second World ⁷_____. He started writing ⁸_____ in 1953. Six ⁹_____ have played the ¹⁰_____ of Bond in films. The most recent is Daniel Craig.

2 Look quickly through the text. Find the name of the man in the photo and his organisation.

1 The man's name is _____ .
2 His organisation is called _____ .

The most famous Bond villain

Ernst Stavro Blofeld is a fictional character who has appeared in seven James Bond films. Several different actors have played the part. In the earliest films, the audience never sees Blofeld's face – only his hands as they stroke a white Persian cat. We see his face for the first time in *You Only Live Twice*.

In the films and in the novels, Blofeld is the leader of a terrorist organization, S.P.E.C.T.R.E., which is trying to dominate the world. In the films, we don't learn very much about his life; we just know that he is a cold, evil and very powerful man who is an enemy of the British Intelligence Service and in particular James Bond. However, Ian Fleming gives us a lot more information in the novels.

Fleming tells us that Blofeld was born on 28th May, 1908 in Gdynia, Poland. His father was Polish and his mother was Greek. Blofeld was a student of economics and history at the University of Warsaw, and then studied engineering at the Warsaw Technical Institute. Later, he got a job with the Polish government. In the Second World War, he secretly worked for both sides and after the war, he moved to South America. He started S.P.E.C.T.R.E. by bringing together the most violent and dangerous criminals in the world.

3 Read the text. Answer the questions.

1 In how many Bond films does Blofeld appear?
_____

2 What pet has Blofeld got?
_____

3 In which film do we first see Blofeld's face?
_____

4 What is S.P.E.C.T.R.E. trying to do?
_____

5 Where was Blofeld born, according to the novels?
_____

6 In which city did Blofeld study?
_____

7 Which side did Blofeld work for during the Second World War?
_____

8 Where did Blofeld go after the war?
_____

4 Number the events of Blofeld's life in the correct order.

☐ He worked for the Polish government.
☐ He moved to South America.
☐ He studied economics.
☐ He started S.P.E.C.T.R.E.
☐ He worked for both sides in the war.
☐ He studied engineering.

●●●●● **CHALLENGE!** ●●●●●

Think of characters from other films. Write information in the chart.

Film(s)	Genre	Character
'Doctor No' and six other James Bond films	action film	Ernst Stavro Blofeld, leader of S.P.E.C.T.R.E.

4D GRAMMAR
(not) as ... as, too, enough

I can use different structures to make comparisons.

1 Look at the information about Jeff Smart and Hannah Brown. Then write sentences using *as ... as* or *not as ... as* and the adjectives in brackets.

(young) Jeff Smart isn't as young as Hannah Brown.

1 (tall) _____
2 (heavy) _____
3 (rich) _____
4 (successful) _____
5 (busy) _____

2 Now write sentences comparing yourself with Jeff Smart or Hannah Brown.

1 (young) _____
2 (tall) _____
3 (heavy) _____
4 (rich) _____
5 (busy) _____

3 Complete the sentences with *enough* and the adjectives and nouns in brackets.

1 Karen isn't __tall enough__ to reach that cupboard. (tall)
2 Ben isn't _____ to ask Kim for a date. (confident)
3 We haven't got _____ to make pancakes. (milk)
4 It isn't _____ to play tennis. (warm)
5 I never have _____ to watch TV. (time)
6 Is your English _____ to visit Britain? (good)

4 Rewrite the sentences using *too* or *enough* and the opposite adjective from the box. Don't change the meaning!

| ~~early~~ generous impatient old popular short |
| slow wet |

1 We're too late to see the start of the film.
We aren't early enough to see the start of the film.

2 I'm too young to see that horror film.
_____

3 These jeans aren't dry enough to wear.
_____

4 His car isn't fast enough.
_____

5 He's too mean to pay for my ticket.
_____

6 The film wasn't long enough.
_____

7 He's too unpopular to win the award.
_____

8 She isn't patient enough to wait.
_____

Jeff Smart

Age	32
Height	172 cm
Weight	75 kg
Money	$52 million
Success	2 awards
Work	2 days a week

Hannah Brown

Age	26
Height	172 cm
Weight	65 kg
Money	$12 million
Success	2 awards
Work	5 days a week

5 Write *as* or *than*.

1 Today isn't as cold _____ yesterday.
2 Are girls more hardworking _____ boys?
3 You didn't get up as early _____ me.
4 *Spiderman 2* is more boring _____ *Spiderman 1*.
5 I'm not as stupid _____ you think I am.
6 Are you as confused _____ me?

●●●●● CHALLENGE! ●●●●●

Complete these common English similes with words in the box. Can you think of similar expressions in your language?

| ABC a bat a bee ice lightning a mouse |
| a picture a tree |

1 He's as cold as _____ .
2 She's as pretty as _____ .
3 He's as quiet as _____ .
4 She's as quick as _____ .
5 He's as blind as _____ .
6 She's as busy as _____ .
7 It's as easy as _____ .
8 He's as tall as _____ .

Similar expressions in your language:
_____
_____
_____
_____

Sofia Coppola

I can understand a profile of a famous film director.

Revision: Student's Book page 38

1 Complete the sentences with words from the box.

> audiences   awards   director   documentary   drama
> film industry   ~~film-making~~   full-length   screen

1 You can study __film-making__ at some universities in the UK, but you won't necessarily get a job in the _____ when you finish.
2 A _____ needs to have interesting characters and a good story.
3 Action films are more exciting when you see them on a big _____.
4 The famous film _____, Martin Scorsese made a _____ about the singer, Bob Dylan.
5 Sometimes, a film is very popular with _____ but doesn't win any _____.
6 Walt Disney made the first _____ animated film in 1937.

2 Read the text about Sofia Coppola quickly. Which paragraph contains information about:

1 her work as an actress? ____
2 her private life?   ____
3 her work as a director? ____

A

Sofia Coppola was born in New York, USA, in 1971 and appeared in her first film, *The Godfather*, in 1972. (She played the part of a baby boy!) As she grew older, she appeared in several other films. However, she was never very successful as an actress, and in 1990 received two joke awards called 'Razzies', one for Worst New Star and one for Worst Supporting Actress.

B

Today, Sofia is better-known (and more successful) as a director. She wrote and directed a short film in 1998 and made her first full-length film, *The Virgin Suicides*, in 1999. That year, she won an MTV Movie Award for Best New Film-maker. In 2003, she wrote and directed her most successful film, *Lost In Translation*, and won an Academy Award for the script.

3 Choose the best answer.

1 As an actress, Sofia's first part was
  A as a boy. ☐
  B as a young girl in The Godfather. ☐
  C in the worst film of 1990. ☐
  D as a young woman. ☐
2 She received two 'Razzies' because
  A she was in several films. ☐
  B she wasn't a very good actress. ☐
  C she was very young. ☐
  D she was a new star. ☐
3 *The Virgin Suicides* was the name of Sofia's
  A first film. ☐
  B short film. ☐
  C first full-length film. ☐
  D most successful film. ☐
4 She won an Academy Award as
  A a writer. ☐
  B an actress. ☐
  C a director. ☐
  D a joke. ☐
5 Two members of Sofia's family are big names in the film industry: her
  A father and daughter. ☐
  B brother and sister. ☐
  C husband and mother. ☐
  D father and cousin. ☐

4 What happened in Sofia Coppola's life on these dates?

1971 _____
1972 _____
1990 _____
1998 _____
1999 _____
     and _____
2003 _____

     and _____

C

Sofia grew up surrounded by people from the film industry because she is the daughter of the famous film director, Francis Ford Coppola. She is also the cousin of actor Nicolas Cage. In 1999, she married film director Spike Jonze but the marriage ended in 2003. Many people in Hollywood believe that she is now in a relationship with Quentin Tarantino – another famous director!

1 Write the questions in the correct order. Then tick the best answers.

1 repeat / you / please / Could / that / ?

_____

  A Yes. I said, 7 o'clock. ☐
  B Thank you. ☐

2 screen / is / Which / it / ?

_____

  A *War of the Worlds*. ☐
  B Screen 2. ☐

3 number / Can / have / your / I / card / ?

_____

  A 03/07 ☐
  B 4657 2192 9383 7126 ☐

4 date / What's / expiry / the / ?

_____

  A 04/08 ☐
  B 4637 6273 4824 2784 ☐

5 book / I / Can / tickets / the / for / U2 concert / ?

_____

  A That's £50. ☐
  B I'm afraid it's sold out. ☐

GLITZY CINEMAS

Film Guide

11–18 March

Screen 1 **Charlie and the** **Chocolate Factory** Certificate PG	14.00 16.00 18.00	**Tickets** Adults: £5.50 Children (under 15), OAPs: £4	
Screen 2 **King Kong** Certificate 12A	17.00 20.00 22.00		
Screen 3 **Madagascar** Certificate U	11.00 13.30 15.30	**Box Office** Tel: 986545 **Book online at** www.GlitzyCin.com	
Screen 4 **Mr & Mrs Smith** Certificate 15	19.00 21.00		

2 Read the film guide and the information about UK film certificates. Then answer the questions.

1 I'm 13 and my brother is 11. Which films can we see together?

_____

2 I'm 14 and my sister is 12. Which films can we see together?

_____

3 I'm 15 and my brother is 13. Can we see *Mr & Mrs Smith*?

_____

4 I'm 16 and my friend is 15. Can we see *Mr & Mrs Smith*?

_____

3 Imagine you are going to see one of the films on the film guide. Make notes.

1 How many tickets? ___ (adults ___, children ___)
2 Which film? _____
3 Screen: _____
4 Which showing? _____
5 Total price: £ _____

4 Complete the dialogue using your notes from exercise 3.

Clerk Hi. Can I help?
You Yes, I'd like ___ tickets for _____ , please.
Clerk Sure. Which showing: _____ or
  _____ ?
You _____ .
Clerk Adults or children?
You _____ .
Clerk OK. So, that's _____ for
  the _____ showing of _____ .
  That'll be £ _____ .
You OK. Here you are. Which is screen is it, please?
Clerk Screen _____ .
You Thanks.

UK film certificates

U = Universal: suitable for everybody, including young children.

PG = Parental guidance: suitable for everybody, but some parts may not be suitable for young children.

12A = Children under 12 can only see this film with an adult.

15 = Only people age 15 and older can see this film.

18 = Only people age 18 and older can see this film.

Preparation

1 Read the review. Match the headings (1–4) with the paragraphs (A–D).

1 The story ☐
2 Susan's overall opinion ☐
3 Background information about the film ☐
4 Other aspects of the film ☐

Pirates of the Caribbean: At World's End
by Susan

A One of my favourite films is *Pirates of the Caribbean: At World's End*. It's an adventure film, starring Johnny Depp and Keira Knightley, and it's the third film in the series.

B The story is set in an imaginary world of pirates. Elizabeth, Will and Captain Barbarossa rescue Captain Jack Sparrow from a monster called 'The Kraken'. However, they then face the evil Davy Jones and a Chinese pirate called Sao Feng.

C The special effects were really amazing, especially the terrifying face of Davy Jones. The acting was excellent too, in spite of the fact that the screenplay wasn't very good. I especially liked Keira Knightley, and Bill Nighy, who played the part of Davy Jones.

D Like the other films in the series, it is full of action and really exciting, although I think the second film in the series was a bit better. Nevertheless, I thoroughly recommend it.

2 Read the review again. Write T (true), F (false) or NG (not given).

1 There are two other films in the *Pirates of the Caribbean* series. ____
2 The film is set in the real world. ____
3 The acting was better than the screenplay. ____
4 Susan wasn't keen on the music. ____
5 This film is a very different from the other films in the series. ____

3 In the review underline the following phrases for expressing contrast.

1 although
2 however
3 in spite of the fact that
4 nevertheless

4 Add the words in the box to the sentences below. Join them with phrases from exercise 3. Sometimes two answers are possible.

> Brad Pitt wasn't very convincing
> ~~I didn't like some of the songs~~
> I really enjoyed this one
> it was supposed to be a horror film
> they spent a lot of money on them

1 Overall the music was quite good,
   although I didn't like some of the songs.

2 The acting was very good.
   _____

3 I don't usually like romantic comedies.
   _____

4 The special effects weren't very good,
   _____

5 The film wasn't very scary,
   _____

Writing task

5 In your notebook write a review of a film you liked or didn't like. Use the Writing Bank on page 104 to help you. Write 130–150 words and follow this plan:

Paragraph 1: Introduction
• name of film, type of film, actors

Paragraph 2: The story
• What happens? Is it gripping? Is it convincing? What about the ending?

Paragraph 3: Other aspects of the film
• the acting, the music, the special effects, the screenplay, the stunts, the location, etc.

Paragraph 4: Your overall opinion
• why you liked / didn't like it

> ### Check your work
> **Have you**
> ☐ written four paragraphs?
> ☐ used some phrases for expressing contrast?
> ☐ written 130–150 words?
> ☐ checked grammar, spelling and punctuation?

Extra Practice

Read the clues and complete the crossword.

CLUES

Across (→)

2 *Shrek* and *Madagascar* are _____ films.

5 Who's _____ tallest boy in the class?

8 The film was very scary – we were really _____.

12 'That's £8'.
'Here you are.'
'£10. Thank you. Here's your _____.'

14 'Do you want to go out this evening?'
'No. I'm _____ tired.

15 The opposite of *entertaining* is _____.

17 The children were very _____ when they got their Christmas presents.

18 Who's _____ intelligent, Ben or Cathy?

Down (↓)

1 'I'd like tickets for one 17-year-old and two 13-year-olds.'
'That's one _____ and two children.'

2 My little sister is really _____. She repeats everything I say!

3 This is the _____ interesting book I've ever read.

4 In your opinion, is *Troy* scarier _____ *Gladiator*?

6 He isn't old _____ to see that film. He's only 12 years old.

7 'That'll be £20, please.'
'Could you _____ that, please?'
'That'll be £20.'

8 I don't like science _____ films.

9 Do you like romantic _____?

10 The comparative form of *funny* is _____.

11 The comparative form of *bad* is _____.

13 Is Diana as tall _____ Susan?

16 I'd like to _____ a ticket for *Batman 5*, please.

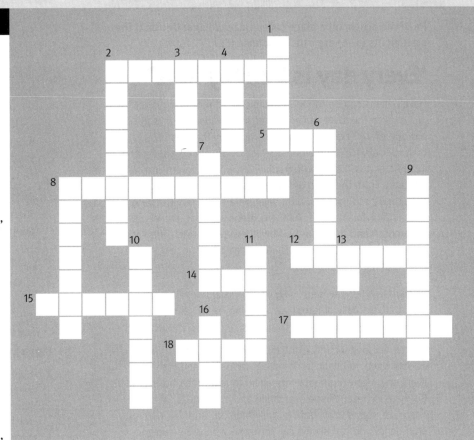

I CAN ...

Read the statements. Think about your progress and tick (✓) one of the boxes.

✳ = I need more practice.   ✳✳ = I sometimes find this difficult.   ✳✳✳ = No problem!

	✳	✳✳	✳✳✳
I can talk about different types of film. (SB p.34)			
I can make comparisons. (SB p.35)			
I can talk about a famous film character. (SB p.36)			
I can use different structures to make comparisons. (SB p.37)			
I can understand a profile of a famous film director. (SB p.38)			
I can buy tickets for a concert or film. (SB p.40)			
I can write a review of a film. (SB p.41)			

Your score [   ] /20

EXAM TASK – Reading

Read the article on a place called Hazel Village. Decide if the statements (1–6) are true (T) or false (F).

'Every day is Sunday here'

Hazel Village can be found in the middle of the countryside, just outside the town of Gloucester, in England. The village is a group of 140 homes – a small community that has been built specially for people over the age of 55. On an afternoon in summer it is like a photograph. Everywhere is quiet and peaceful. From the big mansion at the centre of the village to the houses and flats around it, everywhere is silent. The park is beautifully maintained. All the gardens are neat, the lawns are smooth and tidy, and the flowerbeds pretty and carefully weeded. The speed limit is 20 kilometres per hour, and there is no graffiti at the bus stop.

'Every day is Sunday here,' says Barry Wilson happily. 'I really love it. It's a totally different way of living, really calm and relaxed.'

For the Wilsons security is the most important thing. In a normal town you hear stories about vandalism and crime every day. Many old people are afraid to leave their houses. But here in Hazel Village everything and everyone is safe. There are nurses who work in the village day and night. In an emergency you can always call someone who will be able to help you. There are no gates to the village, it is open to the public, but strangers don't often come to visit.

So there are pros but there are also some cons. You gain peace, quiet and security, but you lose some of the energy of a real town. Ivan Jameson is 95% happy with life in Hazel Village. But he has one complaint: 'There are no young people here. Everyone is old.'

'It's sometimes a sad place,' says his wife Annabel. 'We're all elderly people, and residents do die.' The residents of Hazel Village have to find their own energy, without the distractions of children and young people. But there is plenty to do, and people feel closer to each other. In a real town old people can feel isolated and forgotten. Hazel Village is pleasant and calm, and the residents feel at home there.

Of course, no-one wants to see the village as an exclusive refuge for the old and wealthy. But realistically, that is what it is. Nobody is poor and nobody behaves badly or breaks the law. There is no vandalism and no noise at night. There are no big families with lots of noisy children. It's certainly true that life is calm and peaceful here, and I admit that often I find screaming children and badly behaved teenagers annoying, but yet there is something missing in Hazel Village. The town feels a bit strange without the lively, energetic mix of residents you find outside.

		T	F
1	The article says there are advantages and disadvantages to life in Hazel Village.		
2	In Hazel Village there are only houses and entertainment for people over 55.		
3	Sometimes angry teenagers and muggers walk the streets of the village.		
4	The disadvantage of Hazel Village is there is not much excitement.		
5	There are no nurses for the old people.		
6	The author's intention is to encourage people to live in Hazel Village.		

PREPARATION: Listening

1 Read the instructions. What kind of programme are you going to hear?
2 Read the multiple-choice answers and underline the key words. Think about the difference in meaning between the answers.

EXAM TASK – Listening

🎧 LISTENING 2 **Listen to the interview with an actress called Sally Wilson. Choose the best answer, A, B or C.**

1 Sally Wilson decided to become an actress when she was
  A sixteen. B fifteen. C seven.

2 After she left drama school she wanted to be
  A a musical actress.
  B a theatre actress.
  C a film actress.

3 Her first role
  A came as soon as she moved to Hollywood.
  B wasn't an important film but it helped her to start.
  C attracted attention because the film was so popular.

4 The role in *The Violinmaker's Daughter* was very demanding because
  A she played a disabled woman.
  B she had to learn to play an instrument.
  C it took a long time to make the film.

5 *The Violinmaker's Daughter* was important because
  A she won an Oscar for her music.
  B she made lots of money from the film.
  C she won an Oscar for a film that meant a lot to her.

TIPS: Use of English

- Read the whole text before you decide on the correct form of the verbs.
- Do not think about only the correct form of the verb but also about meaning and use.
- If there is an adverb with the verb in brackets (e.g. *already visit*), think about the correct word order.
- When you have finished, read the text again and check your answers.

EXAM TASK – Use of English

Complete the text with the correct form of the verbs in brackets.

I think I have been very lucky in my life so far, because I have travelled a lot since I [1]_____ (leave) my own country, Canada, in the late 1970s. In the 1980s I [2]_____ (travel) a lot in South America, but I would say that my favourite part of the world is the Indian subcontinent. I [3]_____ (also spend) long periods of time on my own exploring Sri Lanka. Now I have two small sons and so I am not as free to travel for long periods as I once was, but we [4]_____ (already visit) about 15 countries together.

I [5]_____ (originally come) to Britain to study English literature. After finishing my degree, I [6]_____ (find) a job as an editorial assistant in Oxford. Although I am now freelance and live in Cambridge, I do most of my writing for the same publisher who [7]_____ (give) me a job more than 20 years ago. At the moment, I [8]_____ (write) a book on people who decided to take a gap year and travel. I am trying to describe their experience while they were away and I'm also doing some research on how the gap year [9]_____ (change) their lives. I hope the book [10]_____ (appear) in a couple of months.

PREPARATION: Writing a report

Read the instructions and answer the following questions:

- Who are you writing the report for?
- What will you include in each paragraph of your report?

After you write, check your spelling and grammar, and the number of words.

EXAM TASK – Writing

You and your classmates took part in a sports event. Write a report (120–180 words) about it for the school magazine. Include the following points:

- basic information about the event (dates, place, atmosphere)
- a description of the event (disciplines, participants)
- your achievements
- an interesting piece of information about the event

PREPARATION: Speaking

Read the instructions and answer the following questions:

- Prepare vocabulary to describe the photos.
- Look at the Functions Bank on page 101.
- Use the present continuous to describe actions and *there is/are* to talk about what is in the photos.

TIPS

- Before comparing the photos, describe the environment/atmosphere in each of them.
- Describe the people in the photos and say what they are doing.
- Then compare and contrast the photos.

EXAM TASK – Speaking

These two photos show different ways of communicating. Compare and contrast them. Include the following points:

- ways of communicating
- price
- reasons for communicating

Which way of communicating do you prefer? Why?

Picture 1

Picture 2

5 Gifts

A VOCABULARY AND LISTENING
At the shops

I can identify different shops and talk about gifts.

1 Look at the Christmas shopping list. Match the gifts with seven of the shops in the box.

> bakery   bank   butcher's   card shop   chemist's
> clothes shop   computer shop   electrical store
> jeweller's   music shop   newsagent's   post office
> shoe shop   sports shop   supermarket

1   Sarah – earrings _____jeweller's_____
2   Mum – perfume _____
3   Jack – Black Eyed Peas CD _____
4   George – tennis balls _____
5   Laura – T-shirt _____
6   Hannah – webcam _____
7   Dad – bottle of wine _____

2 What can you buy at these shops? Think of at least two examples for each shop and complete the chart.

You can buy ...	and ...	at the ...
stamps	envelopes	post office
		bakery
		card shop
		electrical store
		newsagent's
		shoe shop

●●●●● CHALLENGE! ●●●●●

Which shops do you go to in your town and what do you buy there? Write five more sentences like the example.

I sometimes buy a birthday card at the card shop.

1 _____
_____
2 _____
_____
3 _____
_____
4 _____
_____
5 _____
_____

●●●●● Extension: Collocations: shopping and money

3 Choose the correct verb in the sentences.

1   Do you **sell** / **spend** birthday cakes?
2   I can't **pay for** / **afford** £16.
3   How much do you want to **cost** / **spend**?
4   How much does it **cost** / **charge**?
5   Buy two for £100 and **sell** / **save** £30!
6   Can I **lend** / **borrow** some money from you?
7   Can you **lend** / **borrow** me £3 to buy this magazine?
8   We **charge** / **cost** £5 for replacing watch batteries.
9   Don't forget, you **borrow** / **owe** me £55!
10 'Where did you **pay for** / **buy** that MP3 player?' 'At the electrical store in town.'

4 Complete the dialogue. Use the verbs in the box.

> afford   borrow   ~~buy~~   cost   lend   sell   spend

Julian   What can I ¹ __buy__ my sister for her birthday?

Darren   What about some perfume? There's a chemist's across the road.

Julian   I can't ² _____ perfume. It's really expensive.

Darren   I could ³ _____ you some money.

Julian   Thanks, but I'd prefer not to ⁴ _____ money from you. I'll just make sure I don't ⁵ _____ too much on her present.

Darren   You could buy her a CD. There's a music shop near the station. New CDs ⁶ _____ only £9.99 there.

Julian   That's brilliant!

Darren   They only ⁷ _____ heavy metal CDs, though.

Julian   Ah. She hates heavy metal.

Darren   Why don't you just buy her a sweatshirt?

Julian   OK. Let's find a clothes shop.

Extra Practice

GRAMMAR
Present perfect

I can talk about recent events.

1 Complete the postcard using the present perfect.

Dear Amy

It's now day 3 of our walking holiday in the Alps.
We ¹_____ (be) here since Saturday. We're
really tired because we ²_____ (walk) more
than 100 km! We ³_____ (not stay) at a single
hotel. We ⁴_____ (sleep) in our tent every night,
so we ⁵_____ (save) lots of money.
The mountains are really beautiful – we ⁶_____
(buy) lots of postcards to show you. The nights
⁷_____ (be) cold, so Julie ⁸_____
(not enjoy) it very much!

See you soon

Bill

2 Alison is on holiday in the Algarve. Look at the things she has done. Write questions and answers.

1	swim in the sea ✓	4	read a lot of books ✗
2	spend a lot of money on souvenirs ✗	5	make a lot of new friends ✗
3	try windsurfing ✓	6	go to an Internet café ✓

1 Has she swum in the sea?
   Yes, she has.

2 _____

3 _____

4 _____

5 _____

6 _____

3 Imagine you are Alison on holiday in the Algarve. Write a postcard using the information in exercise 2.

Dear _____

We've been here in the Algarve for a week
now and I'm having a great time.

_____

_____

_____

_____

_____

love
Alison

Helen C
45 Hilli
Oxford
OX2 7
Englan

4 Complete the text. Use the present perfect, affirmative or negative.

Jane Williams is getting married in July. Her
parents are planning the wedding. They
¹_____ (decide) which relatives and friends
they want to invite, but they ²_____
(not send) the invitations. They ³_____
(speak) to the priest and Jane's dad ⁴_____
(find) a hotel for the party. Jane's mum ⁵_____
(make) the cake but she ⁶_____ (not choose)
the flowers yet. They ⁷_____ (not buy) Jane
and her boyfriend a present yet.

5 Write questions with *How long ... ?* Then write true answers with *for* or *since*.

1 you / be / in this class?
   How long have you been in this class?
   I've been in this class since September.

2 your teacher / know / you?

   _____

3 you / live / in your house or flat?

   _____

4 you / study / English?

   _____

5 you / have / your shoes?

   _____

I can talk about special occasions.

Revision: Student's Book page 46

1 Match the special days in the box with the definitions.

> All Saints Day   birthday   Christmas   Easter
> Father's Day   Halloween   Mother's Day   name day
> New Year's Eve   St Nicholas's Day   Twelfth Night
> Valentine's Day   wedding

1 Your _____ is the feast day of the saint who has the same name as you.

2 _____ is 31st December.

3 _____ is 31st October.

4 _____ is a special day to celebrate fathers.

5 Your _____ is the anniversary of your birth.

6 _____ is the festival that celebrates the death and resurrection of Christ.

7 _____ is 6th December.

8 _____ is 5th/6th January, when the three Kings arrived in Bethlehem.

9 _____ is 1st November.

10 _____ is a special day to celebrate mothers.

11 _____ is 14th February.

12 _____ is 24th/25th December.

13 A _____ is the celebration of a marriage.

2 Complete the text using the words in the box.

> celebration   custom   gather   gifts   particularly
> symbolise

HOGMANAY

In Scotland, the biggest [1]_____ of the year is 'Hogmanay'. Hogmanay is the Scottish word for New Year's Eve. On 31st December in Edinburgh, there is an enormous firework display at the castle, and they play live music in the park. Thousands of people [2]_____ in the streets, cafés and bars. Then, at 12 o'clock, church bells ring all over the city.

After midnight, people go 'first footing'. This is a Scottish [3]_____ that dates back hundreds of years. First footing is visiting your neighbours after midnight on New Year's Eve. The visitors must step into the house with their right foot first, to bring good luck. Traditionally the visitors bring three [4]_____: a piece of coal, a piece of 'shortbread' (a Scottish biscuit) and a little whisky. The gifts [5]_____ warmth, food and happiness. If the first person who visits your home after midnight is a man with dark hair, that is [6]_____ lucky!

3 Answer the questions.

1 What does the word 'Hogmanay' mean?
_____

2 What happens at midnight in Edinburgh on 31st December?
_____

3 When do people go 'first footing'?
_____

4 Why must visitors step into the house with their right foot first?
_____

5 What do the gifts symbolise?
_____

6 What kind of first visitor is especially lucky?
_____

4 Complete the phrases with words from the box.

> decorations   fireworks   friends   gifts   a party
> special clothes   special food   special music

1 have _____   5 listen to _____

2 exchange _____   6 put up _____

3 wear _____   7 set off _____

4 eat _____   8 visit _____

●●●●● CHALLENGE! ●●●●●

Read the *Look out!* box. Then choose two special days from exercise 1. Write two sentences about them. Use the phrases in exercise 4 to help you.

Look out!

> We say *at* *Christmas / Easter / Halloween* and *at a wedding*.
> We use *on* with all the other special days.

At Easter we buy chocolate eggs. It is a custom to hide them in the garden and look for them.

1 _____
_____
_____

2 _____
_____
_____

5D GRAMMAR
Present perfect and past simple

I can talk about past experiences and when they happened.

1 Complete the conversations. Use the present perfect or past simple.

Brian   ¹ <u>Have</u> you <u>been</u> (go) camping?
Kim   No, I ² _____ (not have). Have you?
Brian   Yes, I ³ _____ (go) camping last year.
Kim   ⁴ _____ you _____ (have) a good time?
Brian   No, it ⁵ _____ (be) awful.

Brenda   ⁶ _____ you _____ (see) *The Da Vinci Code*?
Matthew   Yes, I ⁷ _____ (have).
Brenda   When ⁸ _____ you _____ (see) it?
Matthew   Last night.
Brenda   ⁹ _____ you _____ (enjoy) it?
Matthew   No, I ¹⁰ _____ (not think) it was very good.

2 Complete the sentences. Use the past simple in one sentence and the present perfect in the other.

1 win
   a Italy _____ the World Cup in 2006.
   b He's happy because United _____ all their matches this year.

2 tidy
   a 'Can you tidy your room?' 'I _____ it this morning.'
   b 'Can you tidy your room?' 'I _____ it.'

3 arrive
   a What time _____ you _____ home last night?
   b '_____ Ben _____?' 'Yes, he's in the living room.'

4 cook
   a Come on, let's eat. Dad _____ dinner.
   b Who _____ this food? It's delicious.

5 meet
   a I _____ lots of interesting people since I arrived.
   b _____ you _____ anyone interesting while you were on holiday?

3 Complete the e-mail. Choose the correct tense: the past simple or present perfect.

Hi Sandra!

I ¹**didn't e-mail / haven't e-mailed** you for ages. Sorry about that! I ²**was / 've been** really busy since my birthday.

Jack and I ³**stopped / have stopped** going out last month. Did you know that? At first I ⁴**was / 've been** really upset about it, but now I'm OK. In fact, I ⁵**just met / 've just met** a really nice boy! He ⁶**asked / 's asked** me out yesterday by text message. I ⁷**didn't reply / haven't replied** yet but I ⁸**decided / 've decided** that I'm going to say yes. We're going to the new cinema. ⁹**Did you ever go / Have you ever been** there? My brother ¹⁰**went / has been** there last month. He says it's great.

E-mail me soon!
Love
Charlotte

4 Complete the text using the past simple and present perfect.

Bill Gates, the founder of Microsoft, is one of the richest men in the world. In 2005 he ¹_____ (earn) $175 million. In 2000, he and his wife ²_____ (start) a charity called the Bill and Melinda Gates Foundation. So far they ³_____ (give) about $28 billion of their fortune to the foundation. Since 2000 the foundation ⁴_____ (spend) billions of dollars on health and education. For example, in July 2000, it ⁵_____ (give) $40 million to scientists working on new ways to fight malaria. In May 2005, it ⁶_____ (provide) more than $11 million for schools and colleges in Chicago. And since 2000, public libraries across the USA ⁷_____ (receive) $250 million to pay for computers and Internet access.

The Empire State Building

I can understand information in a tourist guide.

Revision: Student's Book page 48

1 Match the buildings with the definitions.

| castle | cathedral | City Hall | concert hall | museum | opera house | palace | tower | ~~skyscraper~~ | temple | stadium |

1 A __skyscraper__ is a very tall modern building.
2 A _____ is a large, important church.
3 You can listen to classical music in a _____ or an _____ .
4 A _____ is a place where people worship (usually non-Christian).
5 You can watch sports events at a _____ .
6 In the past, kings and queens often lived in a _____ , but these days, they usually live in a _____ .
7 A _____ is a tall, narrow building.
8 A _____ is a building used by the government.
9 You can look at old and interesting objects or paintings in a _____ .

2 Think of examples of the following buildings (either in your country or in other countries).

1 a museum _____
2 a cathedral _____
3 a castle _____
4 a tower _____
5 a palace _____
6 a stadium _____

3 Complete the text with the words in the box.

| building | dominates | floors | spectacular | tallest | tourist attractions | workers |

The Empire State Building

The Empire State Building is probably the most famous skyscraper in the world. For forty-one years, it was also the ¹_____ building in the world, and it has starred in over 90 films!

Construction started on 22nd January 1930, and 500 ²_____ completed the work in just one year and 45 days. It stands 448 metres high and has got 102 ³_____ , 73 lifts and 6,500 windows.

4 Choose the correct answers.

1 The Empire State Building
   A is the tallest building in the world. ☐
   B was the tallest building in the world. ☐
2 It was built in
   A the 1920s. ☐   B the 1930s. ☐
3 It took
   A just under a year to complete. ☐
   B just over a year to complete. ☐
4 A plane crashed into the building because
   A the weather was bad. ☐   B it was dark. ☐
5 Taipei 101 is
   A taller than the Empire State Building. ☐
   B shorter than the Empire State Building. ☐
6 Every night they shine
   A a light from the top of the building. ☐
   B different coloured lights, depending on the occasion. ☐

●●●●● **CHALLENGE!** ●●●●●

Write a short text about one of the buildings in exercise 2 (about 50 words). Include the following information:
- Where is it?
- What happens there?
- When was it built?

_____
_____
_____
_____

On 28th July 1945 a plane crashed into the Empire State Building. The pilot couldn't see where he was going because it was very foggy. Fourteen people died, but luckily the ⁴_____ didn't fall down.

The Empire State Building is no longer the tallest building in the world – eight buildings are taller. The tallest is Taipei 101, in Taiwan, which stands 509 metres high. However, the Empire State Building still ⁵_____ the New York skyline. Every evening they shine white light on the building, but the colours often change: red and green at Christmas, gold during Oscar week, and they turned the lights off on the anniversary of Pope John Paul II's death.

The building is one of New York City's most popular ⁶_____ . Millions of visitors have climbed to the top to enjoy the ⁷_____ views over the city – even King Kong came to visit!

EVERYDAY ENGLISH
Buying clothes

I can go shopping for clothes.

1 Label the pictures with the words in the box.

> jacket   jeans   shirt   skirt   sweatshirt   top
> tracksuit   trainers   T-shirt

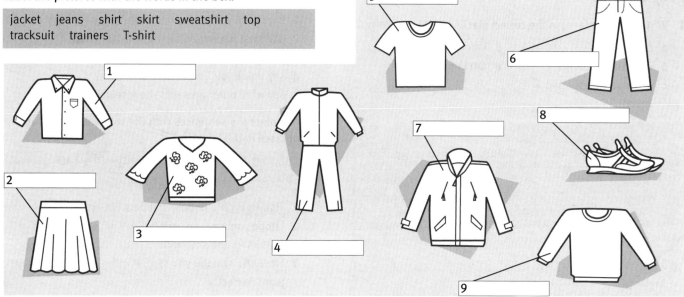

2 Write the prices in numbers.

1 Four pounds seventy-five £4.75
2 Ten pounds _____
3 Six ninety-nine _____
4 Three pounds ten _____
5 One fifty _____

3 How do we say these prices? Write the words.

1 55p fifty-five p
2 £2.25 _____
3 99p _____
4 £23 _____
5 £4.49 _____

4 Put the letters in the correct order to complete the conversations.

1 a Is it OK?
   b No, it doesn't __fit__ very well. (t i f)
2 a That shirt is cheap.
   b Yes, it's in the _____. (l e s a)
3 a I'd like to buy this shirt.
   b Sure. Come over to the _____. (l i t l)
4 a I'll take this top, please.
   b That's £9, please ... Thanks. And £1 _____.
      (a n c h g e)
5 a How much is this T-shirt?
   b The _____ is on the label. (r i p e c)
6 a I'd like to change this top. I bought it last weekend.
   b Of course. Have you got the _____? (e c e r t p i)

5 Complete the questions with the words in the box.

> about   help   much   size   try

1 Can I _____ you?
2 What _____ are you?
3 Can I _____ them on?
4 How _____ these ones?
5 How _____ are they?

6 Use the questions in exercise 5 to complete the conversation.

Shop assistant	1 _____
Andy	Yes, I'm looking for some black jeans.
Shop assistant	2 _____
Andy	Small.
Shop assistant	3 _____
Andy	Yes, they look nice. 4 _____
Shop assistant	£30.
Andy	5 _____
Shop assistant	Sure. The changing rooms are over there.

WRITING

An informal letter

I can write an informal thank-you letter.

Preparation

1 Write the lines (a–e) in the correct places (1–5) in the letter.

a Love,   d Kate
b Dear Uncle George,   e 4th January
c 45 Whitehouse Road
  Bristol BS22 6TH

1 _____
  _____
                    2 _____
3 _____

Paragraph 1

a _____ the
Maroon 5 CD that you sent me for Christmas. It's fantastic!
They are my favourite band.
b _____. I've already
downloaded it onto my MP3 player and I listen to it all the
time.

Paragraph 2

c _____. My
sister came home from university and our grandparents came
to stay. d _____.
Mum and Dad gave me some jewellery and I got a new dress
too. I'm going to wear it on New Year's Eve.

Paragraph 3

e _____,
and that we see you soon. Thanks again for the CD!

4 _____

5 _____

2 Complete spaces a–e in the three paragraphs of the
thank-you letter with the phrases in the box.

> Thank you very much for   It's just what I wanted
> I got lots of great presents   We had a really good Christmas
> I hope you and Aunt Joan are well

3 Look again at exercise 1. In which paragraph did the writer:

1 say thank you for the first time? 1
2 say what happened on the special occasion? ___
3 say what the present is and say something about it? ___
4 say thank you again? ___
5 say what other presents she received? ___

4 Complete the sentences with the colloquial words and
phrases in the box.

> brilliant   go with   gorgeous   given ... back   mates
> plane   reckon   the States

1 Thanks for the Robbie Williams CD – it's _____.
2 I hope you enjoyed your holiday in _____.
  Thanks for the souvenir!
3 I love the sweater you sent, it will _____ my new
  jeans perfectly.
4 Thanks for the MP3 player. All my _____ think it's
  really cool.
5 The scarf you gave me is _____. Thank you very
  much!
6 The DVD was great. I _____ it's his best film so far.
7 Thanks for the guidebook. I'm going to read it on the
  _____.
8 I love the cook book! I borrowed it from the library but
  I've _____ it _____.

Writing task

5 In your notebook write a thank-you letter. Use the Writing
Bank on page 102 to help you. Write 130–150 words and
follow this plan.

Paragraph 1
• Say thank you. Say what the present is and say something
  about it: What's it like? Why do you like it? Have you used it?

Paragraph 2
• Say what you did on the special occasion. Say what other
  presents you received.

Paragraph 3
• Say thank you again.

Check your work

Have you
- [ ] laid out the letter correctly?
- [ ] included all the information?
- [ ] written 130–150 words?
- [ ] checked grammar, spelling and punctuation?

 Extra Practice

SELF CHECK 5

Read the clues and complete the crossword.

CLUES

Across (→)

2 _____ have you lived here?

4 Can I try _____ these jeans, please?

5 How much money does he _____ on clothes?

7 Have you _____ been snowboarding?

9 small – _____ – large – extra large

11 'I'd like this jumper, please.' 'You can pay for it at the _____ .'

12 I bought a new CD player at the _____ shop in town.

16 The past participle of *write* is _____ .

17 This top doesn't _____ . It's too big.

18 You can buy stamps at the _____ office.

Down (↓)

1 'How much does this DVD _____ ?' '£15.'

2 'Have you phoned your mum?' 'No, I _____ .'

3 Pete isn't here. He's _____ to the beach for the day.

6 She bought a magazine at the _____ .

8 I've had this watch _____ Christmas.

10 'Have you been to Japan?' 'Yes, I have.' 'When _____ you go there?'

13 The price is on the _____ .

14 The past participle of *meet* is _____ .

15 I lent my brother £10 last week and £5 yesterday. So now he _____ me £15.

17 I've been at this school _____ two years.

Your score ____ /20

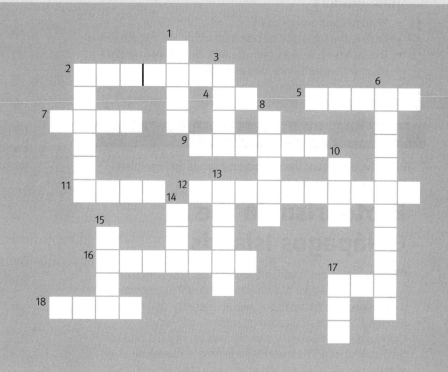

I CAN ...

Read the statements. Think about your progress and tick (✓) one of the boxes.

✱ = I need more practice.   ✱✱ = I sometimes find this difficult.   ✱✱✱ = No problem!

	✱	✱✱	✱✱✱
I can identify different shops and talk about gifts. (SB p.44)			
I can talk about recent events. (SB p.45)			
I can talk about giving gifts on special occasions. (SB p.46)			
I can talk about past experiences and when they happened. (SB p.47)			
I can understand information in a tourist guide. (SB p.48)			
I can go shopping for clothes. (SB p.50)			
I can write an informal thank-you letter. (SB p.51)			

TIPS: Reading

- Read the text quickly to find out what it is about.
- Look at the table and decide what information is missing.
- Use words or phrases from the text. Do not try to replace them with expressions that mean the same.
- Check that the completed sentences are grammatically correct, and also check your spelling.

EXAM TASK – Reading

Read the text about the Galápagos Islands and complete the information in the table.

Ecotourism in the Galápagos Islands

The Galápagos Islands are situated over 600 miles off the coast of Ecuador and close to the Equator. These volcanic islands are considered a 'natural laboratory' and have become a favourite destination for scientists and nature lovers. Unfortunately, the Galápagos Islands have become the victim of their own 'success'. Their worldwide fame has brought too many tourists who often behave no better than if they were visiting a zoo – feeding the animals inappropriate foods and throwing litter around.

Since the Galápagos Islands receive over 100,000 visitors each year, protective measures have been taken to protect the islands and their ecosystem. The population on the four inhabited islands (Santa Cruz, Isabela, San Cristobal, and Floreana) is controlled through strict migration policies regulating the number of permanent residents, and limiting the stay of temporary residents (tourists, volunteers, and external workers) to six months.

For visitors, conservation regulations mean that visits to the islands' National Park territory are limited to about 50 sites, available only during daylight hours (6 a.m. to 6 p.m.) and subject to park rules and guidelines. All groups that visit the National Park must be accompanied by a qualified guide approved by the National Park. The visitors must follow the marked trails and never leave them. If they do so, they may destroy nests without realising it, because marine iguanas nest in the sand.

Park rangers and guides ask tourists to check their clothes and luggage for insects and seeds, because no live material should be transported to the islands. If visitors travel with their pets, they have to leave them in the hotel. Animals living on the islands should not be touched. A young sea lion will be abandoned by its mother, for example, if she smells the scent of a human on her young. The same applies to young birds.

Litter of all types must be kept off the islands. Only certain items can be disposed of at sea in selected areas. Do not buy souvenirs or objects made from plants or animals of the islands (with the exception of articles made from wood). Among such articles are turtle shells, sea lion teeth, and black coral.

The islands	• 1 Scientists think of the Galápagos as a(n) _____. • 2 Only _____ of the islands are inhabited. • 3 Some tourists do not realise they are not in a(n) _____ and cause a lot of damage.
Visiting the islands and the National Park	• 4 Visitors to the islands are not allowed to stay longer than _____. • 5 The National Park can only be visited during _____. • 6 Don't go to the National Park without a(n) _____. • 7 Don't walk off the _____.
Care for the environment	• 8 Check your belongings for _____ and _____. • 9 Don't take your _____ with you. • 10 Don't touch the _____. • 11 Don't drop _____. • 12 Buy gifts made only from _____.

TIPS: Use of English

- Read the dialogue to the end before you start to write.
- Read the answer to each question carefully and think about how to form the verb.
- Read the completed dialogue again. Check the verb forms, word order and spelling.

EXAM TASK – Use of English

A TV interviewer is talking to Helen Wilson, a young tennis champion. Complete the dialogue.

I: Helen, you are playing very well at the moment. How often ¹ *do you train*?

H: Well, I do some training nearly every day to keep fit.

I: Of course. And how old ² _____ when you started playing?

H: I think I was about five or six.

I: That's quite young. Who ³ _____ your teacher?

H: My mum – she is still a very good player.

I: And when ⁴ _____ your first competition?

H: I won the Schools Championship when I was eleven.

I: So, how many tennis cups ⁵ _____ so far?

H: Well, I'm not sure, but I think I've won about ten or twelve cups up to now.

I: That's brilliant! And what about your next match? Where ⁶ _____ to play?

H: I'm going to play the French under-16 champion in Paris.

TIPS: Listening

- Read the questions and options carefully before you listen.
- Think about who the people are and where they are for each extract.
- Don't choose an answer because you hear the same words in the recording. Focus on the meaning to choose the correct answers.

EXAM TASK – Listening

🎧 **LISTENING 3** Listen to four people talking in different situations. Choose the best answer, A, B or C.

1 What problem did the man have in the library?
   A He didn't pay his fine.
   B He couldn't borrow any more books.
   C He returned his books late.

2 Why didn't the man and woman see the play?
   A The woman didn't want to go to the theatre.
   B There weren't any tickets left.
   C The music wasn't very good.

3 Where is the woman going?
   A To visit her brother in Paris by train.
   B To catch a bus home.
   C To visit her brother in Paris by plane.

4 What does the girl say about surfing?
   A She hasn't got a life saver certificate or a surfboard.
   B She's a strong swimmer but she hasn't got her own surfboard.
   C She's a strong swimmer but she thinks surfing is dangerous.

PREPARATION: Writing an informal letter

Read the instructions and answer the following questions:

- What kind of letter should you write: formal or personal?
- What information do you need to include?
- How long should your letter be?

Use the Writing Bank on page 102 to help you.

TIPS

- When you have finished, make sure you have included all the required information.
- Count the words and adjust the length, if necessary.
- Check your letter carefully for mistakes.

EXAM TASK – Writing

You are at an international youth camp. Write a letter (120–180 words) to your friend from the USA, including the following points:

- information about the camp
- how you found out about it
- the length of your stay
- activities at the camp
- other participants and their nationalities – describe an interesting person
- your opinion of the camp

PREPARATION: Speaking

Read the expressions and complete the table.

	Making suggestions	Accepting suggestions	Rejecting suggestions
Why don't we/you (do sth)?	✓		
That's a good idea, but …			
How about (doing sth)?			
Sure, why not?			
(Yes,) I'd be glad to.			
It would be great if we (did sth).			
I'd love to, but …			
Well, I'd rather (do sth).			
Yes, that would be excellent.			
Sounds good to me.			
That could be fun.			
Do you fancy (doing sth)?			

EXAM TASK – Speaking

Your penfriend is planning to visit you for two weeks next summer. He/She (your examiner/partner) phones you to find out about the holiday. Discuss when would be the best time for him/her to come and what you think he/she should do while staying with you. (There are a few ideas below but you can add your own suggestions, too.) Think about the following points:

- time available/needed for the activity
- costs involved
- preparation needed in advance

THINGS TO DO IN THE SUMMER

- see the sights of the city
- go on a boat trip
- check out what exhibitions are on at the museums
- go to the summer music festival
- other ideas?

A VOCABULARY AND LISTENING
Useful gadgets

I can describe electronic devices.

1 Look at the pictures and complete the puzzle. Find the word that isn't illustrated (↓).

Crossword grid:
1 D _ _ P _ _ _ R
2 _ B _ _ P _ _
3 _ G _ _ L _ _ O
4 H _ _ D _ _ _ D _
5 _ S
A
6 M _ 3 _ _ Y
7 C _ L _ _ R
8 S _ _ L _ T
9 C _ _ D
10 G _ _ C
11 V _ _ C _ R
12 P _ _ B _ C P _ _

2 Complete the advertisements. Use words from the box.

CD   copy   easy   ~~gadget~~   miss   record   video tapes

1 This is a fantastic ¹ gadget ! It's really small – not much bigger than a ² _____. You can listen to all your favourite CDs wherever you are!
ONLY £19.99

2 Have you still got lots of old ³ _____ at home? For only £30 you can buy the VR100 and watch them. You can also record all your favourite TV programmes. You'll never ⁴ _____ them again!

3 This gadget is simply the best. Use it with your TV and play all your favourite games. It's really ⁵ _____ to use.
FANTASTIC PICTURES, FANTASTIC SOUND!

4 Use the CR-550 to ⁶ _____ all those special times with your friends. You can then ⁷ _____ the films you make onto DVDs and watch them on your TV.
Special offer: £149.99

3 Which electronic devices are the advertisements for?

1 _____   3 _____
2 _____   4 _____

●●●●● **Extension:** Phrasal verbs

4 Complete the chart. Use verbs from the box.

pick   put   switch   take   turn

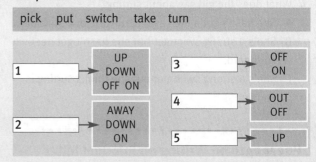

1 _____ → UP DOWN OFF ON
2 _____ → AWAY DOWN ON
3 _____ → OFF ON
4 _____ → OUT OFF
5 _____ → UP

5 Complete the sentences with verbs from exercise 4.

1 She couldn't read the newspaper, so she took out her glasses and _____ them on.
2 I can't hear the music. Can you _____ it up?
3 Don't leave your coat on the floor. _____ it up!
4 _____ off your sweatshirt if you're hot.

6 Complete the sentences. Use *away*, *down*, *on*, and *out*.

1 Remember to take _____ the old batteries.
2 Put _____ that knife. It's dangerous.
3 Turn _____ the TV. I want to watch the news.
4 I'll wash the plates if you put them _____ in the cupboard.

 Extra Practice

I can make predictions, offers, promises and decisions.

1 Choose *will* or *going to* in these predictions.

1 I think England **will** / ~~are going to~~ win the next World Cup.
2 Kate **will** / **is going to** have a baby.
3 Look at that car! It's going too fast. It **'ll** / **'s going to** crash!
4 Do you think you **'ll** / **'re going to** live in the same town all your life?
5 I think it **'ll** / **'s going to** rain next week.
6 I've bought Tom a games console for his birthday. I'm sure he **'ll** / **'s going to** like it.
7 He's running past the goalkeeper. He **'ll** / **'s going to** score a goal! Yes, he's scored!

2 Complete the conversations with the verbs in the box. Use *will* or *going to*.

get	~~have~~	lend	look for	turn down	watch

1
A Would you like a pizza or a burger?
B I <u>'ll have</u> a pizza, please.

2
A I've decided to buy a new digital camera.
B Really? What make _____ you _____?

3
A Why are you turning on the DVD player?
B Because I _____ _____ a film.

4
A Oh, no! My mobile phone isn't working.
B Don't worry, I _____ _____ you mine.

5
A That stereo is too loud.
B Sorry, I _____ it _____.

6
A Has Ben got a place at university?
B No. He _____ a job.

3 Complete the conversation. Use *will* or *going to* and the verbs in brackets.

Sam ¹ <u>Are you going to come</u> (come) to the cinema with me and Rob tomorrow?

Ellie No, I'm not. I ² _____ (spend) the evening with my sister.

Sam Really? Well, why don't you both come to the cinema? I ³ _____ (get) two extra tickets.

Ellie We've got other plans. We ⁴ _____ (have) dinner in a pizza restaurant.

Sam What time ⁵ _____ you _____ (go) out?

Ellie About 8.00. Why?

Sam Maybe we can meet later. I ⁶ _____ (phone) you after the film.

Ellie OK.

●●●●● **CHALLENGE!** ●●●●●

Write down:

1 two things you intend to do this weekend
<u>This weekend I'm going to</u> _____
_____
_____

2 two things you don't intend to do this weekend
_____
_____

3 two predictions
_____
_____

CULTURE
Mobile phones

I can talk about how people use mobile phones.

Revision: Student's Book page 56

1 Complete the sentences with the nouns in the box.

> bill   handset   number   ringtone   text message
> voice calls   wireless headset

1 Who pays the _____ for your mobile phone calls?
2 'Hello, is that James?'
  'No, my name's Peter.'
  'Sorry. I dialled the wrong _____.'
3 If I don't answer my phone, send me a _____.
4 This _____ is really old. I want to upgrade it.
5 When you use your mobile phone in the car, you should use a _____.
6 I don't like texting people. I prefer talking to them, so I usually make _____.
7 I downloaded a great _____ last night. Listen.

2 Match the phrases in A with the phrases in B. Then use the expressions to complete the sentences.

A		B	
1	is addicted to	a	a texting competition
2	stay in touch with	b	about £10 on texts
3	pay	c	my friends
4	take part in	d	my phone bill
5	spend	e	text messaging

1 My dad says he'll _____ because I haven't got any money.
2 My brother _____. He sends about 50 messages a day!
3 I use my mobile to _____.
4 My brother is a really fast texter. Next week he's going to _____. I hope he wins.
5 They _____ every month. Do you think that's a lot of money?

3 Read the text. What can you do with 3G phones? Tick (✓) the boxes.

download songs ☐   record TV programmes ☐
make coffee ☐   access the Internet ☐
watch TV ☐   print letters ☐
listen to the radio ☐   download videos ☐
send and receive e-mails ☐ play music ☐

The only gadget you'll ever need

Nowadays you can make voice calls, send text messages, take photos and record video clips with most mobile phones. However the latest 3G phones can do much more than that. 3G stands for 'third generation'. With 3G phones you can do many things that you normally do on a computer. For example, you can access the Internet and send and receive e-mails. On some models you can even type letters and download them onto your PC in order to print them. You can download songs from the Internet and play them on your phone, and you can also listen to the radio. It's also possible to download videos, e.g. episodes of your favourite TV programme or the highlights of a football match. The most recent phones actually allow you to watch TV so you never need to miss your favourite programmes. Mobile phone manufacturers are hoping that in the future a mobile phone is the only gadget you'll ever need!

●●●●● CHALLENGE! ●●●●●

Can you write these text messages in normal English?

1 WHERE RU?
  Where are you?
2 DO U WNT 2 GO OUT 2NITE?
  _____
3 W8 4 ME @ THE PRK
  _____
4 THX 4 YR TXT MSG
  _____
5 CU L8R
  _____

1 Write zero conditional sentences using the words.

1 people / usually smile / at you / you / smile / at them
People usually smile at you if you smile at them.

2 I / eat / a lot of chocolate / I feel ill
_____

3 plants / die / they / not get / enough water
_____

4 you / freeze / water / it / turn / to ice
_____

5 I / can't / sleep / I / drink / too much coffee
_____

6 I / not do / my homework / my teacher / get / annoyed
_____

7 you / turn off / the lights / you / use / less electricity
_____

8 you / download / songs / you / can / listen to / them on your MP3 player
_____

●●●●● CHALLENGE! ●●●●●

Complete the sentences with information that is true of you. Use the zero conditional.

1 If I go to bed late, _____

2 If I forget to do my homework, _____
_____

3 If I don't have breakfast, _____
_____

4 I get annoyed if _____

5 If I eat too much, _____
_____

6 I feel sad if _____

may, might and *could*

2 Write sentences, with *may* or *might*.

> She loves me. She loves me not. She loves …

1 It's possible that she loves me.
  She might love me.

2 It's possible that I'll buy a digital radio.
_____

3 It's possible that my mobile phone is broken.
_____

4 It's possible that he'll want to borrow my camcorder.
_____

5 It's possible that my parents will buy me a new games console.
_____

3 Make the sentences in exercise 2 negative.

1 _____
2 _____
3 _____
4 _____
5 _____

4 Complete the answers. Use *may*, *might* or *could* and your own ideas.

1 'What are you doing on Saturday evening?'
  'I'm not sure. _____
  _____,'

2 'Where are you going on holiday next summer?'
  'I haven't decided yet. _____
  _____,'

3 'What are you going to buy your mum for her birthday?'
  'I'm not sure. _____
  _____,'

4 'What are you going to do when you leave school?'
  'I don't know yet. _____
  _____,'

5 'What are you going to have for dinner this evening?'
  'I don't know. _____
  _____,'

Revision: Student's Book page 58

1 Complete the phrases with nouns from the box.

> copies   damage   diseases   the environment
> the future   ~~predictions~~   a robot

1 make ___predictions___
2 build _____
3 cure _____
4 repair _____
5 make _____
6 predict _____
7 damage _____

2 Use the phrases from exercise 1 to complete the sentences.

1 It's difficult to ___make predictions___ about the future.
2 Nanobots can _____ to the human body.
3 Scientists are trying to _____ that can do the housework.
4 If nanobots escape, they could _____.
5 'Do you think that robots will one day take over the world?'
  'I don't know. I can't _____!'
6 Doctors are continually developing new ways to _____.
7 Some scientists are worried that nanobots will be able to _____ of themselves.

4 Answer the questions.

1 What prediction from 30 years ago are people repeating now?

_____
_____

2 Why will there be fewer accidents in the future?

_____
_____

3 What kinds of job will robots be able to do in the future?

_____
_____

4 What are some scientists worried about?

_____
_____

5 What are the most extreme predictions?

_____
_____

5 Read the text again and underline two positive predictions and two negative predictions about robots.

6 Which predictions do you think are more likely to come true: the positive or the negative? Give a reason.

I think the _____ predictions are more likely to come true because _____

_____.

3 Complete the text with the words in the box.

> change   control   inventors   nightmare   predictions
> the world   worries

Robot Revolution

'Are you tired of cleaning the house? Tired of cooking? Don't worry. Soon, domestic robots will do all the boring jobs while you relax.' People were saying this thirty years ago, but it hasn't happened. Now they're saying it again, but this time it's probably true. Robots will [1]_____ our lives. But will this new technology be a dream or a [2]_____?

Some scientists believe that robots will make [3]_____ a better place. We will build robots that can do all the dangerous and difficult jobs. There'll be fewer accidents and life will be safer. They think that [4]_____ will develop robots that are incredibly intelligent and that will do the jobs of doctors, pilots and scientists.

However, other scientists have serious [5]_____ about robot technology. They believe that intelligent robots might be difficult to [6]_____. What happens if robots don't follow instructions? The most extreme [7]_____ say that robots will destroy the human race and possibly the entire planet.

6F EVERYDAY ENGLISH
Arranging to meet

I can make arrangements to meet somebody.

1 Complete the dialogues with the words from the box.

| bookshop | cinema | coffee bar | drink | see you |
| top floor | | | | |

a Would you like to go to the ¹_____? There's a new thriller on.

b Great! I'll ²_____ by the stairs.

a Hi Tom. I'm bored. Do you fancy a ³_____?

b OK. I'll meet you in the ⁴_____ in twenty minutes.

a My favourite writer is speaking tonight at the ⁵_____.

b Really? What time?

a At seven o'clock on the ⁶_____.

2 Match the halves of the questions.

1 What are you ...	**a** meeting up in town?
2 Do you fancy ...	**b** are we going to meet?
3 Where do you ...	**c** meet at the cinema?
4 What ...	**d** time?
5 Why don't we ...	**e** want to meet?
6 Where exactly ...	**f** up to?

1 What are you up to? _____
2 _____
3 _____
4 _____
5 _____
6 _____

3 Complete the conversation with the words in the box.

| fancy | how | idea | inside | it's | later | meet |
| much | see | up | want | you | | |

Alice Hi, Steve. ¹_____ Alice.

Steve Hi, Alice. How are ²_____?

Alice Fine. What are you ³_____ to?

Steve Nothing ⁴_____. Why?

Alice Do you ⁵_____ meeting up for a pizza?

Steve Sure. That's a great ⁶_____. What time?

Alice Well, I'm playing tennis with Bethany now, so ⁷_____ about after the game – at five o'clock?

Steve Five o'clock? That's fine. Where do you ⁸_____ to meet?

Alice We could ⁹_____ at the pizza restaurant.

Steve Where are we going to meet exactly? ¹⁰_____ or outside?

Alice Outside.

Steve OK. I'll ¹¹_____ you there at five.

Alice Great. See you ¹²_____. Bye!

4 Imagine you are phoning a friend to arrange a meeting. Decide:

- a time to meet _____
- a place to meet _____
- the exact meeting point _____

5 Complete the conversation with Simon. Use your notes from exercise 3.

You Hi, Simon. It's _____.

Simon Hi, _____. How are things ?

You Fine. _____?

Simon Nothing much. Why?

You _____?

Simon Sure. That's a great idea. What time?

You _____

Simon That's fine. Where shall we meet?

You _____

Simon OK. See you there in an hour. Where exactly are we going to meet?

You _____

A formal letter

I can write a letter of complaint.

Preparation

1 Match the parts of the formal letter (a–h) with the numbers on the diagram (1–8).

```
                              1   xx xxxxxxxx xx
                                      xxxxxxxx
                                  xxxxxxxx xxxx

  3   xxxxxx xxxxx          2   xx xxxx xxxx
      xxxxxxxx xxx
      xxxxxxxxxxx

  4   xxxx xx xxxxxxxx

  5   xxx xxxxxx xxx xxxxxxx xxx xxxxx xxx xxxxx xxx xxx
      xxxx xxxx xx xxxxx xxxx xxxx xxxxx xxxxx xxx  xx

      xxxx xxxx xx xxxxx xxxx xxxx xxxxx xxxxx xxx  xxxx
      xxxx xxxx xx xxxxx xxxx xxxx xxxxx xxxxx xxx  xxxxx
      xxxx xxxx xx xxxxx xxxx xxxx xxxx xxxxx xxxxxx xx

      xxx xxxxxx xxx xxxxxxx xxx xxxxx xxx xxxxx xxxxxx
      xxxx xxxx xxxxx xxxxx xxxx xxxx xxxx xxxxx xxx

  6   xxxxx xxxxxxxx

  7   xxxxxx xxxxxx

  8   xxxxxx xxxxxx
```

a	the date	☐
b	your name – printed	☐
c	*Yours faithfully* (or *Yours sincerely*)	☐
d	*Dear Sir or Madam* (or *Dear* + name)	☐
e	your address	1
f	the name and address of the person you are writing to	☐
g	your signature	☐
h	the main part of the letter	☐

2 Complete the sentences with the prepositions in the box.

| about   from   to   to   to   with   with |

1 I am writing _____ complain _____ the TV I have just bought.
2 I would like to report a fault _____ the computer that I bought _____ your website.
3 I am returning the games console _____ you _____ this letter.
4 I look forward _____ hearing from you.

3 Write the words in the correct order to make set phrases from a letter of complaint.

1 to / fault / I / writing / am / report / a
_____

2 to / returning / I / am / the / camera / you
_____

3 would / the / you / could / grateful / repair / if / modem / I / be
_____

4 DVD player / could / send / please / me / new / a / you / ?
_____

5 together with / enclosing / I / the digital radio / am / the receipt
_____

6 look / I / forward / you / from / to / hearing
_____

Writing task

4 In your notebook write a formal letter of complaint about a new gadget. Use the Writing Bank on page 102 to help you. Write 130–150 words and include this information.

Paragraph 1
• Explain why you are writing. Say what the gadget is called. Say when and where you bought it.

Paragraph 2
• Say exactly what the problem is.

Paragraph 3
• Say that you are returning the gadget. Ask the company to repair it or send you a new one.

Check your work

Have you
☐ laid out the letter correctly?
☐ included all the information?
☐ used formal language?
☐ written 130–150 words?
☐ checked grammar, spelling and punctuation?

Extra Practice

SELF CHECK (6)

Read the clues and complete the crossword.

CLUES

Across (→)

5 'What are you up _____?'
   'Nothing much.'
6 My new _____ takes great photos.
8 Look at those dark clouds. It's
   _____ to rain.
9 I need to ring home. Can I borrow your
   _____ phone?
12 Turn _____ the music! I'm trying to
   read!
13 'What would you like?'
   'I _____ have a pizza. please.'
14 We've got _____ TV, so we can get
   lots of channels.
18 'Do you _____ going to the cinema?'
   'Yes, great idea.'

Down (↓)

1 We use _____ to talk about
   intentions.
2 We use _____ for offers and
   promises.
3 I'm rather tired, so I _____ not go
   out this evening.
4 I made a video of our holiday with my new
   _____ .
5 If you're hot, why don't you _____
   off your sweatshirt?
7 I _____ happy if I get good marks in
   my exams.
9 Bob loves animals. He _____
   become a vet.
10 _____ water reaches 0°C, it freezes.
11 'Where are we going to meet?'
   '_____ meet at the café.'
15 If I wash the plates, can you put them
   _____ , please?
16 _____ on the radio. There's a
   programme I want to hear.
17 _____ don't we meet up later for a
   coffee?

Your score ___ /20

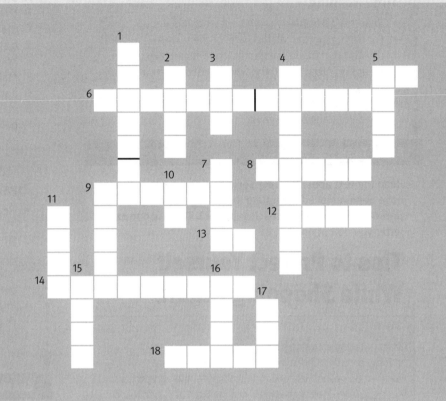

I CAN ...

Read the statements. Think about your progress and tick (✓) one of the boxes.

✳ = I need more practice.   ✳✳ = I sometimes find this difficult.   ✳✳✳ = No problem!

	✳	✳✳	✳✳✳
I can describe electronic devices. (SB p.54)			
I can make predictions, offers, promises and decisions. (SB p.55)			
I can talk about how people use mobile phones. (SB p.56)			
I can talk about outcomes and possibilities. (SB p.57)			
I can understand an article in detail. (SB p.58)			
I can make arrangements to meet somebody. (SB p.60)			
I can write a letter of complaint. (SB p.61)			

TIPS: Reading

- Read the text quickly to find out what it is about.
- For each gap, read all the parts of the text (A–I) and find the one that fits in the gap both grammatically and in meaning. Always read the whole sentence (or the whole paragraph) to check that it makes sense.
- Remember that there is always one part of the text that doesn't fit any of the gaps.

EXAM TASK – Reading

Read the text about Internet security. Some parts of the text have been removed. Complete the text by deciding which part of the text (A–I) fits each gap (1–8). There is one extra letter you do not need.

Tips to Protect Yourself While Shopping Online

Tip 1

Make sure you are using a secure server and browser with industry security standards before you enter credit card information online. First look at the address in the address bar and ¹_____.Then look at the bottom of the Internet window and make sure there is a closed padlock.

Tip 2

Use companies you know. Anyone can open ²_____ and be gone tomorrow. Here are some things to research ³_____ with an unknown company.

⁴_____ for the company and compare this with information from the domain register.

Check for a return policy.

Check to see if ⁵_____.

Are they a member of Better Business Bureau Online (BBBO)?

Tip 3

When shopping we all hope that we ⁶_____ but sometimes there are problems that arise with what we ordered. Check the company's return policy online before you order, so you will ⁷_____.

Tip 4

Keep information about your order. Also ⁸_____such as return policies, company information, specific product information and warranty information.

Trust your instincts – if it sounds too good to be true … it probably is!

A print out other information you may need
B check that it starts with 'https'
C there have been any complaints
D a store online in minutes
E know what to expect
F Make sure there is contact information
G a well selected password
H get what we ask for
I before doing business

TIPS: Use of English

- Read the text quickly to find out what it is about.
- The words you choose must fit both the grammar and the meaning of the text.
- Read the words before and after the gap and decide what kind of word you need (a noun, an adjective, a verb, etc.).
- Then read all the words in the box. Some of them do not fit grammatically and so they cannot be correct.
- When you have finished, read the text again to check your answers.

EXAM TASK – Use of English

Complete the article about a famous painting with the words in the box. There is one extra word that you do not need to use.

cleaning shows every highest later marriage marry seen sent some common

In 1968 a New York art dealer, Ira Spanierman, found a dirty portrait of a man with a beard painted by an unknown Italian artist. He liked ¹_____ of the details in the painting, and decided to pay $325 for it. After ²_____ the painting, experts realised it was by Raphael, the famous Renaissance artist who lived in early 16th-century Italy. The portrait ³_____ Lorenzo di Medici, a prince who was about to ⁴_____ a cousin of François I, the King of France at the time. The portrait was ordered from Raphael as a gift to be ⁵_____ to Lorenzo's bride, as exchanging portraits before a marriage was fairly ⁶_____ then. Lorenzo and his wife died shortly after their ⁷_____ and the portrait had not been ⁸_____ for centuries, until Spanierman found it almost 400 years ⁹_____. During an auction in July 2007, four people fought over the painting, and finally an anonymous millionaire offered the ¹⁰_____ price over the phone. The portrait of Lorenzo Medici was sold for $37.3 million – 100,000 times the price Spanierman paid for it in 1968.

PREPARATION: Listening

1 Read the instructions. How many people will you hear? What will they talk about?
2 Read the statements (1–9), and say whether they are true for you or not.
3 Which do you prefer: small shops or big shopping centres? Why?

EXAM TASK – Listening

🎧 LISTENING 4 Listen to three young people talking about their shopping habits. Match the information (1–9) with the speakers (A Lucy, B Tina, C Pete).

1 only goes to shopping centres to buy things for a computer ☐ L

2 hates all kinds of shops ☐

3 prefers smaller shops ☐

4 finds boutiques very expensive ☐

5 doesn't use the Internet for shopping ☐

6 loves ordering goods on the Internet ☐

7 finds the music in shopping centres irritating ☐

8 thinks that shopping centres are great places to meet friends ☐

9 wants to spend as little time as possible shopping ☐

PREPARATION: Writing a description

Read the instructions and answer the following questions:

• What style and format should you follow?
• What do you have to include in your description?
• How many paragraphs will you need for your text?
• What information should you include in each paragraph?

EXAM TASK – Writing

Last month you moved to a new flat and you have your own room. Write an e-mail (120–180 words) to your friend in Australia and tell him/her about it. Include the following points:

• two pieces of information about the new flat
• the surroundings of the flat
• your new room
• your feelings

PREPARATION: Speaking

Think about these questions:

1 What can you do at your school after lessons?
2 Have you ever taken part in any extra-curricular activities? When? What did you do? Did you enjoy it?
3 Have you ever helped to organise any school activities? If so, how easy or difficult was it? If not, what activities do you think should be organised at your school?

EXAM TASK – Speaking

Your school is planning to introduce some new activities next term. You are at a meeting with the representative of the school (your examiner/partner) to discuss the ideas that have come up so far. Look at the suggestions below and decide which of the activities you think would be best for your school and why. (You can also recommend new ones.) In each case think about the following:

• Why choose this activity?
• How easy/difficult is it to organise? (place, people needed, etc.)
• What costs are involved? (prizes, equipment, etc.)
• What other people/things will be needed? (activity leaders, books, etc.)

Ideas for new activities for next term

• a talent contest
• a new school choir
• a poetry reciting competition
• a dance competition
• a new drama group
• a new judo club
• a new school radio station

7 Cultures and customs

A VOCABULARY AND LISTENING
Body language

I can describe how people greet each other in different countries.

1 Complete the phrases with these verbs: *cross, fold, hold, pat, point, shake.*

1 _____ hands
2 _____ somebody on the back/head/etc.
3 _____ your arms
4 _____ your head
5 _____ at somebody / something
6 _____ your legs
7 _____ hands

2 Write sentences describing the gestures. Use phrases from exercise 1 and words from the box.

beckon   bow   hug   nod   wave

1 <u>They're holding hands. She's</u> _____

2 _____

3 _____

4 _____

5 _____

6 _____

●●●●● **Extension:** Phrasal verbs

3 Complete the P.E. teacher's instructions with the words in the box.

~~down~~   down   over   out   over   round   up   up   up   up

1 Lie <u>down</u>!

2 Turn _____!

3 Sit _____!

4 Stand _____!

5 Put _____ your hands!

6 Lift _____ your foot!

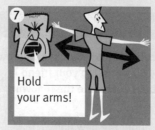
7 Hold _____ your arms!

8 Bend _____!

9 Turn _____!

10 Sit _____!

Extra Practice

7B GRAMMAR

must, mustn't and *needn't*

I can talk about prohibition and necessity.

1 Rewrite the sentences. Use *must* or *mustn't*.

1 In Japan it's important that you don't wear shoes indoors.
In Japan you mustn't wear shoes indoors.

2 In some Muslim countries it's important that women cover their hair.

3 In many Asian countries it's important not to eat with your left hand.

4 In many countries it's important not to point at people with your finger.

5 In American restaurants it's important that you leave the waiter a 15% tip.

6 In the USA it's important not to touch people if you don't know them very well.

7 It's important not to call people after about 10 p.m. unless it's an emergency.

2 Choose the correct word to complete the sentences.

1 He **needn't** / **mustn't** get up early. He can stay in bed.
2 I **mustn't** / **must** go home now. It's very late.
3 We **mustn't** / **needn't** hurry. We've got lots of time.
4 I **mustn't** / **must** forget to phone Sam. He's waiting to hear from me.
5 They **needn't** / **mustn't** go out tonight. They've got a lot of homework to do for tomorrow.
6 You **needn't** / **must** see that film. It's fantastic.
7 She **mustn't** / **needn't** wear those jeans. They're dirty.
8 You **must** / **needn't** shout. I can hear you.

3 Write sentences with *you mustn't* or *you needn't*.

1 It isn't necessary to wear a tie.
You needn't wear a tie.

2 It's important not to be late.
_____

3 It isn't necessary to eat with a knife and fork.
_____

4 Don't wink at women.
_____

5 Don't take off your shoes if you don't want to.
_____

6 It isn't necessary to take a gift when you visit him.
_____

7 It's important not to belch at the table.
_____

8 Don't accept the invitation if you don't want to go.
_____

●●●●● CHALLENGE! ●●●●●

Write sentences about your life at home. Write two with *must*, two with *mustn't* and two with *needn't*.

1 _____
_____
2 _____
_____
3 _____
_____
4 _____
_____
5 _____
_____
6 _____

Extra Practice

Unit 7 • Cultures and customs **61**

Revision: Student's Book page 66

1 Complete the sentences about Thanksgiving with the words in the box.

> charity   harvest   ill   last   parade   tradition
> turkey

1 Americans celebrate Thanksgiving on the _____ Thursday in November.
2 According to American _____, the first Thanksgiving took place in 1621.
3 The Pilgrims became _____ because they didn't know how to grow food in North America.
4 Thanks to the help of two Native Americans, the Pilgrims' first _____ was good.
5 Many people do _____ work – helping poor and homeless people.
6 The most popular food is roast _____ and vegetables.
7 On Thanksgiving day in New York there's a big fancy-dress _____.

2 Complete the text with the words in the box.

> celebrate   come together   occasion   organise   soup
> took place   traditionally

Bonfire Night

Every year on 5th November people in Britain
¹_____ Bonfire Night. They light big bonfires in
their gardens and in parks and ²_____ firework
displays. People sometimes cook potatoes in the fire and
drink ³_____ while they watch the fireworks.
⁴_____, people make a model of a man, called a
'guy', with old clothes and newspaper, and burn him on
the fire. This is because on 5th November 1605, a man
called Guy Fawkes tried to blow up King James I and his
government in London. Guy Fawkes wanted to kill the
king because the king was a Protestant and Guy Fawkes
wanted a Catholic king. Fawkes wasn't successful, and the
first Bonfire Night ⁵_____ in 1606, a year later.
Originally, Bonfire Night was an ⁶_____ on
which people celebrated the fact that Guy Fawkes didn't
kill the king. Nowadays, it is just a festival where family
and friends ⁷_____ to watch a firework display.

3 Answer the questions.

1 What date is Bonfire Night?
_____
2 What do people eat and drink?
_____
3 Traditionally, what do people do with the guy?
_____
4 What did Guy Fawkes try to do?
_____
5 When was the first Bonfire Night?
_____

●●●●● **CHALLENGE!** ●●●●●

Write about a festival in your country. Include in your text answers to some of the questions in the box.

> What is the name of the festival?
> When does the festival take place? What happens? Why
> does it take place? What do people wear? What do they eat?
> Why do you like it?

_____
_____
_____
_____
_____
_____
_____
_____
_____
_____
_____

D GRAMMAR
First conditional

I can talk about a future situation and its consequences.

1 Match the phrases to make six first conditional sentences.

> You'll have seven years of bad luck
>
> If you see a magpie in the morning,
>
> If a man smiles a lot during his wedding,
>
> you won't remember what you've learned.
>
> if you see a spider in your house.
>
> If you wash your hair on the morning of an exam,
>
> if you eat lentils on 1st January.
>
> you'll get good news that day.
>
> You'll make a lot of money during the year
>
> if you break a mirror.
>
> You'll have visitors
>
> his first child will be a girl.

1 You'll have seven years of bad luck if you break a mirror.
2 _____
3 _____
   _____
4 _____
   _____
5 _____
   _____
6 _____
   _____

2 Complete the first conditional sentences.

1 If there __is__ (be) a good film on TV, we __'ll watch__ (watch) it.
2 I _____ (help) you if you _____ (want).
3 If we _____ (not hurry), we _____ (miss) the train.
4 He _____ (not mind) if you _____ (not phone) him.
5 If I _____ (have) time tomorrow, I _____ (help) you with your homework.
6 I _____ (make) you a sandwich if you _____ (be) hungry.

3 Complete the sentences. Use the present simple or *will* and the verbs in the box.

| lie down   not be able   not turn round   ~~not wait~~ |
| open   rain |

1 We __won't wait__ for you if you're late.
2 If it _____ tomorrow, we won't go to the beach.
3 If you _____, you won't see him.
4 You _____ to sleep if you drink too much coffee.
5 You'll feel better if you _____.
6 If you're hot, I _____ the window.

4 Look at the pictures. Complete the first conditional sentences. Use the phrases in the box.

bump his head	squash the cat
get a surprise	~~trip over the bag~~
sit in his dinner	turn into a prince

1 If she doesn't lift her foot up,
   __she'll trip over the bag__ .

2 If he sits down,
   _____ .

3 If she kisses the frog,
   _____ .

4 If he doesn't bend down,
   _____ .

5 If she turns round,
   _____ .

6 If he lies down,
   _____ .

Extra Practice

Unit 7 • Cultures and customs **63**

7E

READING

Unusual festivals

I can understand a description of different cultural traditions.

Revision: Student's Book page 68

1 Complete the sentences with the words in the box.

> at risk   banned   casualties   concerned   horns
> injured   participants   sign up   spectators

1 People who stand in the street during the Thai water throwing festival are _____.
2 The authorities _____ the cheese rolling festival but the tradition soon started again.
3 Every year at the water throwing festival, people are _____ in car accidents.
4 _____ in the bull running need to be very fast runners.
5 _____ at the bull running must stay behind the fences along the road.
6 There were a lot of _____ at the last cheese rolling – 15 people were hurt.
7 If you want to take part in the cheese festival, you don't have to _____ – you can simply join in.
8 If a bull catches you with its _____, you can get badly injured.
9 Some people are _____ about the number of casualties at the water throwing festival.

2 Quickly read the text. True or false?

1 The tomato fight takes place in Spain. _____
2 The police banned the fight. _____
3 Tourists don't travel to the town during the tomato fight.

_____

3 Write questions for these answers.

1 *When / start*? <u>When did la tomatina start?</u>
  In 1945.
2 *Who / stop*? _____
  The police.
3 *How long / last*? _____
  One hour.
4 *When / take place*? _____
  On the last Wednesday in August.
5 *How many / join in*? _____
  About 40,000.
6 *What / happen*? _____
  Everyone gets together and eats and drinks.

●●●●●● **CHALLENGE!** ●●●●●●

Invent an unusual festival. Think of answers to some of the following questions. Write about 40 words.

What is the name of the festival?   What do people do?
What makes it unusual?   What do people wear?
How did it start?   Are there any rules?

_____

Tomato fight

In July 1945, a tomato fight started in the market square of Buñol, near Valencia in Spain. Two young men began to argue and, because they were standing next to a fruit stall, they picked up tomatoes and threw them at each other. Other people joined in but the police soon stopped the fight. The young men had to pay for all the tomatoes that they threw. The following year young people in the town met again at the market square and started another tomato fight. Again, the police stopped the fight, but a tradition began: *la tomatina*. A few years later the local government banned the tomato fight, but the people continued the tradition illegally. In 1959, the fight became legal again, but the participants had to follow two simple rules: they couldn't start throwing tomatoes until a special signal, and they had to stop exactly an hour later. Today, *la tomatina* is a big tourist attraction. It takes place every year on the last Wednesday in August. About 40,000 people join in the fight and throw over 100 tonnes of tomatoes at each other. After the fight everyone gathers in the square and eats and drinks until late in the evening.

EVERYDAY ENGLISH

Making invitations

I can make and accept or decline an invitation.

1 Complete the diagram with words from the box.

~~shopping~~   a barbecue   a football match   a party
basketball   computer games   for a bike ride
friends   lunch in a café   skateboarding
to a rock concert   to the cinema

SOCIAL ACTIVITIES

GO
1 shopping
2
3
4
5

HAVE
7
8
9

PLAY
10
11

MEET
6

WATCH
12

● ● ● ● ● ● **CHALLENGE!** ● ● ● ● ●

How many more social activities can you add?

1 _____   5 _____
2 _____   6 _____
3 _____   7 _____
4 _____   8 _____

2 Complete the sentences with *on*, *at* or nothing.

1 We're having barbeque __on__ Saturday.
2 See you tomorrow _____ five o'clock.
3 I'm going to a party _____ tonight.
4 We're going to the cinema _____ Friday night.
5 The football match starts _____ 8.30.
6 See you _____ Monday.
7 What are you doing _____ tomorrow?

3 Choose the best reply.

1 We're having a party on Saturday night.
   A Really? That sounds fun. ☐
   B That's a shame. ☐
2 See you tomorrow at the cinema.
   A Great. See you next week. ☐
   B Great. See you there. ☐
3 I can't come to the disco with you.
   A Oh, well. Sorry you can't make it. ☐
   B Glad you can make it. ☐
4 Do you fancy joining us?
   A Really? See you later! ☐
   B Yes, I'd love to thanks. ☐

4 Complete the conversations with the sentences in the box. Use each sentence once.

I'd love to, but I can't.   I'm sorry, I can't.
I'd love to, thanks.   Thanks. I'll definitely be
I'm afraid I won't be able   there.
   to make it.   Yes. That sounds great!

1 A We're having a party this evening. Why don't you come along?
   B _____
   A Great. See you there.
2 A I'm going to a football match tomorrow. Would you like to come?
   B _____
   A That's a shame.
3 A We're going shopping this afternoon. Do you fancy joining us?
   B _____
   A Glad you can make it.
4 A I'm having lunch with Chris. Would you like to join us?
   B _____
   A Sorry you can't make it.
5 A We're playing basketball this evening. Do you fancy joining us?
   B _____
   A That's a shame.
6 A I'm meeting Jake at the cinema in half an hour. Would you like to come?
   B _____
   A Great. See you there.

5 Put the lines in the correct order to make a conversation.

☐ **Diana** Really? That sounds fun.
☐ **Diana** I'd love to but I can't.
☐ **Diana** What are your plans for Saturday?
☐ **Diana** I'm going shopping in London with my parents.
☐ **Toby**   I'm going for a bike ride with my sister.
☐ **Toby**   Oh. Sorry you can't make it.
☐ **Toby**   Do you fancy joining us?
☐ **Toby**   That's a shame. Why not?

I can write a note replying to an invitation.

Preparation

1 Put the words in the correct order to make sentences. Write the sentences in the correct place (a–f) in the notes.

1 much / your / thanks / for / note / very
2 be / I'll / there / definitely
3 great / I / a / have / you / picnic / hope
4 be / won't / afraid / I / to / I'm / make / able / it
5 for / party / thanks / birthday / much / invitation / the / to / very / your
6 time / does / what / start / it / ?

Dear Nicola

a *Thanks very much for your note*. It's very kind of

you to invite me to your picnic, but b_____

_____ .

I'm going to visit my cousin in Liverpool that

weekend. It's a shame, because I'd love to come.

Anyway, c_____

_____ .

Love

Joe

Hi William

I got your note. Great to hear from you.

d_____

_____ .

e_____ . I'm

really looking forward to it.

f_____

_____ ?

See you soon.

Kelly

P.S. I'll bring some crisps and biscuits.

---

2 Complete the sentences with the colloquial expressions in the box.

| guess | hear from you | make it | mates | too bad |

1 I'm having a barbecue with my _____ .
2 See you at the party. I'm glad you can _____ .
3 Thanks for your note. It's really nice to _____ .
4 I'm afraid I can't come to the match with you. It's _____ , because I'd love to see Chelsea play.
5 I _____ we'll have a barbecue in the garden if the weather's fine.

3 Add the missing letters to the abbreviations.

1 Bring something to drink, __.g. cola.
2 Let me know a._. a._. if you can come.
3 Give me ring – t_ __. 453890.
4 Thanks very much for the C _ s. Great music!
5 I've got all the food, drink, music, e__c. for the party.

4 Read Victoria's invitation. Underline:

1 expressions that mean *make it* and *mates*.
2 abbreviations that mean *phone number*, *road* and *please reply*.

It's my birthday next Saturday and I'm going to the cinema with a few friends. Do you fancy joining us? We're going to see 'The Sentinel'. I'm really looking forward to it. Hope you can come with us.

Victoria

RSVP   29 Mill Rd.   Tel. 6451453

Writing task

5 In your notebook write a note accepting Victoria's invitation, and a note declining her invitation. Use the Writing Bank on page 102 to help you. Write 40–50 words and include this information.

1 Accept the invitation
- Thank her for the invitation.
- Accept the invitation.
- Add a P.S. to ask a question about the occasion.

2 Decline the invitation
- Thank her for the invitation.
- Decline the invitation.
- Give your reason for declining it.

Check your work

Have you
- [ ] included all the information?
- [ ] used some colloquial expressions?
- [ ] used some abbreviations?
- [ ] written 40–50 words?
- [ ] checked grammar, spelling and punctuation?

 Extra Practice

Read the clues and complete the crossword.

CLUES

Across (→)

1 She _____ down and picked up the magazine from the floor.

2

6 What will you do _____ she doesn't phone you?

7 Do you _____ up when a teacher comes into the classroom?

10 _____ down on that chair.

11 If you're tired, _____ down and go to sleep.

12 It's very late. I _____ go home now.

14 'We're going for a picnic. Do you fancy joining us?'
   'Yes, that _____ great.'

18 You _____ take an umbrella. It isn't going to rain.

19 _____ your hand up if you know the answer to the question.

Down (↓)

1

3 'Can you come to a party at the weekend?'
   'I'm _____ I won't be able to make it.'

4 Do you _____ hands when you meet somebody for the first time?

5 We _____ swim here. It's dangerous.

8 He folded his _____ .

9 'Would you like to come to the cinema with us?'
   'I'd love to, thanks.'
   '_____ you can make it.'

13 When she woke up she sat _____ in bed.

15 'Can you come to the café with us?'
   'I'm sorry. I can't.'
   'That's a _____ .'

16 If I _____ pass my exams, I'll take them again.

17 If it rains, we _____ go out.

Your score /20

I CAN ...

Read the statements. Think about your progress and tick (✓) one of the boxes.

✳ = I need more practice.   ✳✳ = I sometimes find this difficult.   ✳✳✳ = No problem!

	✳	✳✳	✳✳✳
I can describe how people greet each other in different countries. (SB p.64)			
I can talk about prohibition and necessity. (SB p.65)			
I can understand the origins of an American festival. (SB p.66)			
I can talk about a future situation and its consequences. (SB p.67)			
I can understand a description of different cultural traditions. (SB p.68)			
I can make and accept or decline an invitation. (SB p.70)			
I can write a note replying to an invitation. (SB p.71)			

TIPS: Reading

- Read the text quickly to find out what it is about.
- All the statements are correct. You need to match them to the paragraphs that contain the relevant information.
- Sometimes the information is found in more than one paragraph. This is shown by numbers next to the statement; the order in which you write the paragraphs is not important.

EXAM TASK – Reading

Read the article about food at a school. Match the information in the sentences (1–10) to the paragraphs (A–D).

Students demand healthy food

A Students at East Hampton Middle School decided to stop using their cafeteria after seeing the documentary 'Super Size Me'. The protest began when about 150 students and their parents were shown a film in which the director, Morgan Spurlock, eats only fast food for a month. The film attacks the state for providing schools with unhealthy food, and it was shown as part of a new health and nutrition program at the school.

B 'After seeing the film, some students linked its message about high-calorie, processed foods with the menu in the cafeteria and decided to stop buying meals at school,' said Ginny Reale, the school's health teacher who helps run the health and nutrition program. Other teachers also mentioned the idea in their classes, and word spread through the school, which has 465 students.

C Teachers and students could not say how many people had stopped using the cafeteria, but queues that had stretched out of the lunchroom door were much shorter on a recent Wednesday. After seeing the film, 'we started talking about how our school didn't have the best lunches for us,' said Devon McGorisk, one of the students in the class that began the protest. 'We wrote down a list of the foods that we wanted.' That list included more salads, fresh sandwiches, fruit salad, and even sushi.

D There was a meeting with the company that prepares the school lunches and several students presented a list of demands. After the meeting, yogurt was added to the menu, but not much else. Although the cafeteria serves salads, sandwiches and fruit, students and teachers said the healthiest options usually run out quickly. Because the lunch period is only 20 minutes – common in schools throughout the area – students often avoid the long queues for the meals and go into the faster and cheaper snack bar where they can get cookies, bagels and sugary drinks.

Healthy meals are not provided in sufficient numbers.	1 _____
Students' decisions were influenced by a film.	2 _____ 3 _____ 4 _____
Students watched the film together with their parents.	5 _____
Some teachers supported the students in their protest.	6 _____
The number of students who stopped eating in the cafeteria is unknown.	7 _____
Students suggested what should be sold in the cafeteria.	8 _____ 9 _____
Students often buy their lunches somewhere else.	10 _____

TIPS: Use of English

- Read the text quickly to find out what it is about.
- Read each sentence to the end and decide what kind of word you need for each gap (a noun, a verb, an adjective, or an adverb?).
- When you have finished, read the whole text again to check your answers.

EXAM TASK – Use of English

Complete the text with the correct form of the words in brackets (1–10).

One of the best outdoor activities is rock-climbing. When you are climbing, you focus on your moves and you can't think about everyday problems. You are in a ^{1}_____ (difference) world and it's a great ^{2}_____ (feel). And as soon as you reach the top, you get a ^{3}_____ (wonder) sense of achievement. If you are ^{4}_____ (interest) in this sport and looking for ^{5}_____ (inform) on rock-climbing, there are several websites on the Internet.

There are many types of rock-climbing like ^{6}_____ (tradition) climbing, sport climbing, top rope climbing or bouldering. Bouldering is the ^{7}_____ (new) of them. It involves climbing rocks, glaciers or large decorative stones at shopping centres. The sport was ^{8}_____ (introduce) about ten years ago as a way to practise certain moves again and again. It can be ^{9}_____ (danger) and you should have some ^{10}_____ (train) to do it. Since its introduction, it has evolved into a challenging sub-sport of climbing and has its own superstars.

TIPS: Listening

- Read the sentences carefully before you listen.
- Listen to each recording and pick out the false information. It can appear anywhere in the sentence.
- Check your answers to make sure your corrections make sense.

EXAM TASK – Listening

🎧 LISTENING 5 Listen to four recordings about superstitions. Each of the statements contains some false information. Underline the wrong word and write the correction.

Recording 1

1 The little <u>boy</u> starts to cry because the
hamster died. _____*girl*_____

2 The mirror in the bathroom fell and broke. _____

Recording 2

3 The man went fishing last Sunday. _____

4 He caught six fish before his luck changed. _____

Recording 3

5 The woman was superstitious about not finishing making her lunch. _____

6 She heard the superstition from her grandfather. _____

Recording 4

7 The traffic is going to make the man late for his meeting. _____

8 The man had a dream about sitting in an empty office. _____

TIPS: Writing a note

- Read the instructions and decide on the style of writing to use. Use the Writing Bank on page 102 to help you.
- Think of the language you need for each point in the task.
- When you have finished, check your grammar and spelling and that you have included all the key information.

EXAM TASK – Writing

You are living abroad and sharing a flat with a student from another country. You share the housework and it's your turn to do the shopping. You have to go out and you won't have time to go to the supermarket. Write your flatmate a note (70–80 words) including the following points:

- inform him/her about the situation
- ask him/her to do the shopping
- tell him/her what to buy (3–5 things)
- tell him/her where to find the money for the shopping

EXAM TASK – Speaking

The following pictures show different kinds of jobs. Compare and contrast them. Include the following points:

- Which of the two looks more like a summer job?
- Can you imagine yourself doing either as a summer job or for a career?
- Have you done any summer jobs?
- What are your plans for your career?

Picture 1

Picture 2

8 What if...?

A VOCABULARY AND LISTENING
Global issues

I can talk about global problems.

1 Find 11 more global issues in the word square and write them below.

Q	W	A	Z	E	W	E	R	J	N	M	F	G	T	Y	U	I
F	A	M	I	N	E	P	A	S	R	A	C	I	S	M	D	F
G	R	H	J	D	K	L	Z	X	C	V	B	N	G	M	N	Q
R	Z	W	S	A	X	E	D	C	R	C	F	V	L	T	G	B
Y	H	N	U	N	J	M	I	T	K	H	O	L	O	P	M	H
N	B	V	C	G	X	Z	L	E	K	I	J	H	B	G	F	O
D	S	A	P	E	O	I	U	R	Y	L	T	R	A	E	W	M
T	H	E	A	R	M	S	T	R	A	D	E	P	L	M	N	E
J	I	U	H	E	B	V	G	O	Y	L	T	F	W	C	X	L
P	D	R	E	D	W	S	Z	R	Q	A	H	G	A	M	B	E
O	Q	W	E	S	R	T	Y	I	U	B	I	O	R	P	A	S
V	S	D	F	P	G	H	J	S	K	O	L	Z	M	X	C	S
E	V	B	N	E	M	L	K	M	J	U	H	G	I	F	D	N
R	S	E	P	C	O	O	U	Y	T	R	R	E	N	W	Q	E
T	F	C	D	I	S	E	A	S	E	U	H	V	G	B	H	S
Y	O	K	N	E	R	D	X	E	S	Z	K	A	J	I	M	S
R	T	Y	U	S	J	P	O	L	L	U	T	I	O	N	N	F

war _____   _____
_____   _____
_____   _____
_____   _____
_____   _____
_____

2 Match these definitions with global issues from exercise 1.

1 Buying and selling guns and other weapons.
_____

2 Having very little money to live on. _____
3 When countries or groups of people fight. _____
4 Illnesses like malaria, HIV, etc. _____
5 Changes in climate caused by CO_2 and other gases.
_____

6 Having no food to eat. _____
7 Violent attacks on a country by people with strong political or religious beliefs. _____

3 Look at the posters. Which of the global issues from exercise 1 are they protesting about?

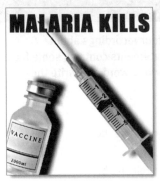

1 _____

2 _____

3 _____

4 _____

●●●●● **Extension:** Word formation: noun suffixes

4 Write the nouns. They all end in *-ation*, *-ion* or *-ness*.

Verb / Adjective	Noun
inform	information
suggest	
sad	
discuss	
dark	
good	
organise	
act	
educate	
happy	

Extra Practice

8B GRAMMAR
Second conditional

I can talk about an imaginary situation and its consequences.

1 Find and join the two halves of second conditional sentences. Add capital letters and punctuation.

> if people didn't drop litter
>
> he'd be healthier
>
> they'd cause less pollution
>
> there would be much less disease
>
> if he had enough to eat
>
> if people didn't kill tigers
>
> if she weren't homeless
>
> the pavements would be cleaner
>
> they wouldn't be an endangered species
>
> if they stopped using their car
>
> if everybody had clean water to drink
>
> she wouldn't sleep on the street

If people didn't drop litter, the pavements would be cleaner.
or
The pavements would be cleaner if people didn't drop litter.

1 _____

2 _____

3 _____

4 _____

5 _____

2 Complete the second conditional sentences with the verbs in the box.

discuss	have	help	know	phone	ring
shake	win				

1 I'd be very surprised if that film _____ an award.

2 If you were in trouble, I _____ you.

3 If I knew her number, I _____ her.

4 I wouldn't answer the phone if it _____ now.

5 If I met a friend in the street, we _____ hands.

6 I'd tell you the answer if I _____ it.

7 If I were you, I _____ it with your parents.

8 We'd save water if we _____ showers instead of baths.

3 Continue the story with more second conditional sentences.

1 If you gave me £200, I'd buy a guitar.

2 (practise every day) If I bought a guitar, I'd practise every day.

3 (play really well) If I practised every day, I'd play really well.

4 (join a band) _____

5 (give concerts around the world) _____

6 (become famous) _____

7 (earn a lot of money) _____

8 (give you £1,000!) _____

4 Answer the questions with your own ideas.

1 What would you buy if you won £5,000 in a competition?
I'd buy _____

2 If you could have a holiday anywhere in the world, where would you go?
_____

3 If you could meet any famous person in the world, who would you choose and why?
_____ because

4 If you saw an alien, what would you do?
_____

5 Who would you take with you if you had two tickets to a great rock concert?
_____

> ●●●●● **CHALLENGE!** ●●●●●
>
> **Can you think of three more endings for this sentence?**
>
> The world would be a better place if ...
> everybody had enough to eat.
>
> 1 _____
> 2 _____
> 3 _____

CULTURE
Going green

I can talk about the environment.

1 Complete the information about the environment. Use the words in the box.

> decompose   improve   oil   organic   ozone
> pesticides   recycles   renewable   ultra-violet
> warming

Plastic bags can take up to 1,000 years to ¹_____. When we go shopping, we should take a bag with us.

The ²_____ layer stops ³_____ light from the sun. It's between 17 and 15 kilometres above the surface of the Earth.

About 90% of the world's energy comes from ⁴_____, coal and gas. One problem is that they are not ⁵_____ – they will eventually run out. Another problem is that when we burn them they cause global ⁶_____.

At the moment the EU only ⁷_____ about 45% of its waste. It wants that figure to be between 50 and 80 per cent.

On non-organic farms, farmers use more than 400 different ⁸_____. These can kill wild animals and birds, and also cause water pollution. If more people bought ⁹_____ food, this would help to ¹⁰_____ the environment.

2 Read the text. Which statement is false?

1 The UK recycles more than Germany and Holland. _____
2 The UK recycles more now than five years ago. _____
3 We throw away a lot of packaging from food. _____

A load of rubbish

In the UK, people are finally starting to listen to the message about recycling. British families now recycle about 22% of their waste. Only five years ago, the figure was about 10%. That's good news for the environment – but there's a lot more to do. Some other European countries, like Germany and Holland, already recycle about 60% of their waste and that's the goal for the UK too.

Households in England produce 25 million tonnes of waste a year. More than half of this is garden waste, paper, cardboard and kitchen waste – which people could recycle. They could also recycle plastic, wood, glass and aluminium cans. In fact, if everybody in the UK recycled all of their drinks cans, there would be 14 million fewer rubbish bins of waste each year.

Recycling isn't the only way to reduce the amount of rubbish we throw away. More than 40% of the waste in our bins is packaging from shopping. If we changed the way we shop, we could easily reduce the amount of waste. For example, street markets and small shops often use less packaging than supermarkets. And of course, if we grew our own fruit and vegetables, there wouldn't be any packaging at all!

3 Answer the questions.

1 How much of their waste do British families recycle now?
_____

2 How much do they recycle in Germany and Holland?
_____

3 How much waste do households in England produce?
_____

4 What eight different things could people recycle?
_____

5 How could we reduce the amount of packaging that we throw away?
_____

●●●●● **CHALLENGE!** ●●●●●

Think of ways that you personally could reduce the amount of rubbish you produce. It could be by recycling, re-using things or changing what you buy.

I could _____

_____

_____

8D GRAMMAR
I wish ...

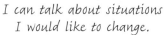

I can talk about situations I would like to change.

1 Complete the dialogues with *I wish ...*

1 **a** I wish I could speak French.

  b Why?

  a If I could speak French, I'd talk to that girl.

2 **a** _____

  b Why?

  a If I didn't have a headache, I'd go out.

3 **a** _____

  b Why?

  a If I had some money, I'd go shopping.

4 **a** _____

  b Why?

  a If my brother wasn't at home, I'd use his computer.

5 **a** _____

  b Why?

  a If the weather was nicer, I'd go to the beach.

6 **a** _____

  b Why?

  a If it was the weekend, I wouldn't have to go to school.

2 Match the thought bubbles with the pictures. Complete them with the correct form of the verbs in the box.

be	have	like	live	know	speak

1 I wish I _____ there.

2 I wish I _____ taller.

3 I wish I _____ the answers.

4 I wish I _____ an umbrella.

5 I wish I _____ pizza.

6 I wish I _____ Japanese.

3 Write sentences starting with *I wish*. Use the past continuous, positive or negative.

1 I'm feeling ill.
  I wish I wasn't feeling ill.

2 You aren't listening to me.
  _____

3 We're losing.
  _____

4 It's raining.
  _____

5 I'm not wearing my glasses.
  _____

6 You're eating all the chocolate.
  _____

7 I'm still doing my homework.
  _____

8 I'm not feeling optimistic.
  _____

9 She's dancing with my friend.
  _____

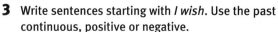

CHALLENGE!

Complete the wishes.

3 wishes to make your own life better ...
I wish _____
I wish _____
I wish _____

3 wishes to make life better for a friend or family member ...
I wish _____
I wish _____
I wish _____

3 wishes to make the world a better place ...
I wish _____
I wish _____
I wish _____

8E

READING

Disaster!

I can understand an article about meteors.

Revision: Student's Book page 78

1 Complete the text about Cumbre Vieja. Use the nouns in the box.

> directions   future   tonnes   tsunami   volcano

Cumbre Vieja is an enormous, active ¹_____ in the Canary Islands. Scientists know that at some time in the ²_____, it will erupt. They are worried that the side of the volcano will collapse and ³_____ of rock will fall into the sea. This would cause a huge ⁴_____ that would travel very fast in all ⁵_____ away from the Canary Islands.

> catastrophe   damage   energy   equipment
> eruption

The wave would have enough ⁶_____ to cross the Atlantic and cause terrible ⁷_____ to the east coast of America. This would be a ⁸_____. Although the scientists can't predict exactly when the volcano will erupt, they are going to put some ⁹_____ on Cumbre Vieja which will give them an early warning of an ¹⁰_____.

2 Look at the pictures and the information below them. Answer the questions.

1 What does picture 1 show?   a m _ _ _ _ _ _ _ _

2 What does picture 2 show?   a c _ _ _ _ _ _

Most meteorites start to burn when they reach the Earth's atmosphere. They get much smaller or disappear.

This crater is from a meteorite that hit the Earth. Until 1903, scientists thought it was the crater of an old volcano.

3 Complete the text with the verbs in the box.

> cause   devastate   fall   happen   hit   predict
> protect   reach   travel

A big hit?

Every year, thousands of rocks from space ¹_____ to Earth. These are called meteorites. Most of these are very small – less than a metre across. They start to burn when they ²_____ the Earth's atmosphere and usually disappear before they ³_____ the ground. (See picture 1.) A few meteorites are too large to disappear when they burn. They ⁴_____ at very high speed – about 60,000 km/h when they hit the ground – and can cause enormous damage. This happened in Arizona about 50,000 years ago and you can still see the crater today. It's called 'Meteor Crater'. (See picture 2.) If another large meteorite hit the Earth today, what would ⁵_____? The explosion would be huge. The meteorite would ⁶_____ everything around it. If it fell into the sea, it would ⁷_____ an enormous tsunami. It would be a catastrophe.

But the good news is that large meteorites don't hit the Earth very often. Also, scientists know about the danger, and can ⁸_____ which meteorites might hit the Earth. It might also be possible to ⁹_____ the Earth by firing a rocket at a meteorite as it came near to the Earth. This would change its direction and save the world.

4 Choose the correct answers.

1 Most meteorites don't hit the Earth because
   A they burn in the Earth's atmosphere. ☐
   B they're too large. ☐

2 'Meteor Crater' appeared when
   A a very large meteorite disappeared. ☐
   B a very large meteorite hit the Earth. ☐

3 If a large meteorite hit the Earth today
   A it would fall into the sea. ☐
   B it would be a catastrophe. ☐

4 The good news is that
   A scientists can't predict when the next meteorite will come. ☐
   B large meteorites don't come very often. ☐

5 We could change the direction of a meteorite
   A if we knew that it was coming nearer. ☐
   B if we fired a rocket at it. ☐

EVERYDAY ENGLISH

Giving advice

I can describe a problem and give advice.

1 Match the verbs in column A with their opposites in column B. Then complete the sentences with the correct form of the verbs.

A	B
lend	take
give	forget
find	break
mend	borrow
remember	lose

1 Dan always _____ my birthday. It's so annoying!
2 I _____ £20 on the pavement this morning. What should I do?
3 Oh no! I've _____ my sister's jacket!
4 Tom _____ my CD player and he hasn't given it back.
5 My boyfriend always _____ me presents but I don't like them.
6 I _____ Dad's digital camera last night.

2 Match the problems (a–f) with the advice (1–6).

a I'm too tired to concentrate at school in the mornings.
b I'm going to miss the final episode of my favourite TV programme.
c A boy keeps phoning my mobile and I don't want to talk to him.
d I want to go on holiday in the summer but I haven't got enough money.
e I've offended my friend. I want to apologise, but he won't talk to me.
f I borrowed a T-shirt from a friend and now I've lost it.

1 ☐ 'I think you should buy her a new one.'
2 ☐ 'I think you ought to tell the phone company.'
3 ☐ 'Why don't you ask a friend to record it?'
4 ☐ 'If I were you, I'd send him a card to say sorry.'
5 ☐ 'I don't think you should stay up so late in the evenings.'
6 ☐ 'In my opinion, you should get a part-time job.'

3 Rewrite the advice from exercise 1 using a different phrase to start each one. Choose from the phrases in the box.

I think you should …	I don't think you should …
I think you ought to …	I don't think you ought to …
If I were you, I would …	In my opinion, you shouldn't …
If I were you, I wouldn't …	In my opinion, you should …
Why don't you … ?	

1 *If I were you, I'd buy her a new one.*
2 _____
3 _____
4 _____
5 _____
6 _____

4 Write the words in the correct order to make a dialogue.

Jack   advice / ask / Can / your / something / about / I / ?
   1 _____
Cath   problem / Sure. / the / What's / ?
   2 _____
Jack   I don't know what to buy my girlfriend for Valentine's Day.
Cath   think / flowers / I / buy / should / you / her / some
   3 _____ .
Jack   good / That's / a / idea
   4 _____ . Thanks!

5 Write two more dialogues like the one in exercise 4. Choose problems from exercise 2. You can invent your own advice, if you prefer.

A   Can I ask _____ ?
B   Sure. What's _____
A   _____
    _____
B   In my opinion, _____
A   Thanks. That's _____

A   Can _____ ?
B   Of course. What's _____ ?
A   _____
    _____
B   If I were you, _____
A   Thanks. _____

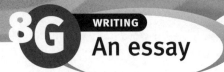

8G WRITING
An essay

I can write an essay on a global issue.

Preparation

1 Complete Martin's essay with the words in the box.

> also   buses   finally   first   make   mind   next

If I ruled my country *by Martin*

If I ruled my country, the ¹_____ thing I'd do is make the government spend more money on public transport. I don't think there are enough trains and ²_____, and they are often overcrowded.

The second thing I'd do is ³_____ school start at 11 o'clock in the morning. I like to go bed late and I find it very difficult to get up early in the morning. I wouldn't ⁴_____ if school went on until six o'clock in the evening.

The ⁵_____ thing I'd do is build more hospitals and employ more doctors. In my view, we have to wait too long to see a doctor at the hospital.

There are ⁶_____ two less serious things I'd do. I'd make CDs much cheaper. In my opinion, they should only cost about £2 each. ⁷_____, I'd ban all serious TV programmes like documentaries, and just have music and sports programmes.

2 Read Martin's essay. How many things would he do?

3 ☐   4 ☐   5 ☐   6 ☐

3 Read Martin's essay again. Find and underline the answers to these questions.

1 Why would he make the government spend more money on public transport?

2 Why would he make school start at 11 o'clock in the morning?

3 Why would he build more hospitals and employ more doctors?

4 Complete the sentences with the words in the box.

> don't think   believe   view   in   convinced   as

1 I am _____ that we should make guns illegal.

2 I _____ that we should pay any taxes.

3 In my _____, the government should ban hunting.

4 I _____ that there's too much crime.

5 _____ I see it, there are too many cars on the roads.

6 _____ my opinion, school shouldn't be compulsory.

5 Put the words in the correct order.

1 make / I'd / shorter. / lessons
   I'd make lessons shorter.

2 the government / make / build / I'd / roads. / more
   _____
   _____

3 sure / there / I'd / homeless / any / weren't / people. / make
   _____
   _____

4 smoking / make / illegal. / I'd
   _____

5 lorries / make / only used / I'd / motorways. / sure
   _____

Writing task

6 In your notebook write an essay about what you would do if you ruled your country. Include some serious and some less serious ideas. Use the Writing Bank on page 103 to help you. Write 130–150 words and follow this plan.

Paragraph 1
• the first thing you would do

Paragraph 2
• the second thing you would do

Paragraph 3
• the third thing you would do

Paragraph 4
• one or two less serious things that you would do

Check your work

Have you

☐ divided your essay into paragraphs?
☐ used phrases from exercise 4 for expressing opinion?
☐ used some expressions with *make*?
☐ written 130–150 words?
☐ checked grammar, spelling and punctuation?

Extra Practice

Read the clues and complete the crossword.

CLUES

Across (→)

1 Selling war planes, ships and guns = the _____ trade

2 I wish I _____ a mobile phone.

6 I'd like some _____ about the museum, please. What time does it open?

7 Pandas, whales and tigers are endangered _____ .

10 If I found €500 in the classroom, I _____ keep it.

12 'I've got an exam tomorrow.'
'Then I _____ think you should stay up late tonight.'

15 'If you're feeling ill, you should go and see the doctor.'
'Thanks. That's a good _____ .'

16 I wish I _____ play the guitar.

18 The streetlamps weren't on so we walked home in _____ .

19 I wish I _____ taller.

Down (↓)

1 Can I ask your _____ about something?

3 I think we _____ to go home now. It's getting late.

4 If I had a lot of money, I _____ buy a motorbike.

5 Verb = discuss. Noun = _____

8 What would you do _____ you didn't have to go to school?

9 Adjective = sad. Noun = _____

11 In my _____ you should apologise for being rude.

13 There's a lot of child _____ in India and Pakistan. A lot of young children go out to work.

14 _____ is behaving badly to people who come from a different country.

17 If I _____ have so much homework, I'd go out with my friends.

Your score ___ /20

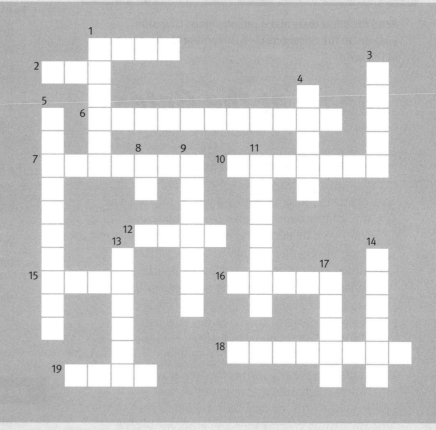

I CAN ...

Read the statements. Think about your progress and tick (✓) one of the boxes.

✳ = I need more practice.   ✳✳ = I sometimes find this difficult.   ✳✳✳ = No problem!

	✳	✳✳	✳✳✳
I can identify global problems. (SB p.74)			
I can talk about an imaginary situation and its consequences. (SB p.75)			
I can talk about the environment. (SB p.76)			
I can talk about situations I would like to change. (SB p.77)			
I can understand an article about a natural disaster. (SB p.78)			
I can describe a problem and give advice. (SB p.80)			
I can write an essay on a global issue. (SB p.81)			

EXAM TASK – Reading

Read the short texts about popular films. Give short answers to the questions (1–6) according to the information in the texts.

Enemy at the Gates

This film was made in English by the French filmmaker Jean-Jacques Annaud. It's the Second World War, and Hitler's army is trying to capture Stalingrad. Khrushchev, in charge of defending the city, is looking for a hero to inspire the soldiers, so political officer Danilov makes the young soldier Zaitsev a hero by publishing his successes in shooting the Germans. Alarmed by the kill rate of the young Russian and the success of Danilov's propaganda, the Germans send one of their best snipers to kill Zaitsev. Some people will enjoy the film because of the suspense of the duel between the German and the Russian soldiers. For others, the fantastic special effects and haunting photography of a city torn apart by war will be the main attraction. But what appealed to me personally was to see how well the film showed the ruthless way war leaders use innocent people.

THE MATRIX

Is this the best film of all time? It's certainly one of my top movies ever. It appears to be a typical American action blockbuster, and in many ways it is. The cool costumes were clearly thought up to appeal to the fashion-conscious young target audience. The science fiction plot and setting is a perfect opportunity for those wild computer-generated special effects. The story is full of those conspiracy theory twists and turns which have proven to be a box office success over and over again. And if you like blood and guts, you'll find plenty of dead bodies in the film. It has everything the young filmgoer could want, so it is no surprise that it has turned into such a great cult movie. What is surprising is that the ideas expressed in the film are so deep and interesting that several teachers have used it in their university philosophy courses.

Enemy at the Gates

1 Where is Hitler's army located in the film?
Outside Stalingrad.

2 Who is trying to find a person to inspire Russian soldiers?
_____

3 Besides the special effects, what helped the film to impress audiences?
_____

The Matrix

4 What did the film-makers hope a young audience interested in fashion would like in the movie?
_____

5 What is guaranteed by the conspiracy theory twists and turns in the film?
_____

6 What has the film become as a result of its popularity with young people?
_____

EXAM TASK – Use of English

Read the text about a stay in Alaska. Write the missing words (1–15). Use only one word in each gap.

I have been in Alaska ¹_____ about a week now, so I've settled in and I'm doing my volunteer work at the environmental centre. Alaska ²_____ really beautiful and the landscape is amazing. I have ³_____ seen any moose yet, or bears, but I think I will sooner ⁴_____ later, because moose walk onto the roads all the time. ⁵_____ is a festival tomorrow and a midnight baseball game, which I'm ⁶_____ to participate in.

I'm staying in a log cabin, ⁷_____ is pretty cool. It has got a loft and a ladder leading up to it, which makes up for the fact that I have ⁸_____ running water. This is the real Alaskan experience! I was surprised that lots of houses here don't have running water or electricity.

I ride a bike to and from work ⁹_____ day. It takes me half ¹⁰_____ hour to get there. The camp where I work started two days ¹¹_____. This week I'll be looking ¹²_____ five-year-old kids. I have ¹³_____ take them to various places and, together with ¹⁴_____, I learn ¹⁵_____ lot about the local environment. I am really enjoying my time here, thanks to the people who are so kind.

TIPS: Listening

- Read the instructions and the questions carefully to find out what the recording is about.
- Listen carefully to the recording, because the words you hear are not the same as those in the statements.
- If the statement is true, you will hear some information that supports the statement.
- If the statement is false, you will hear some information that contradicts the statement.

EXAM TASK – Listening

🎧 LISTENING 6 Listen to a report on New Orleans and Hurricane Katrina. Decide whether each statement is true (T) or false (F).

		T	F
1	The speed of winds was 130 km an hour.		
2	No one expected the consequences of the hurricane to be very bad.		
3	Jim Greengrass comes from New Orleans.		
4	The levees protect the city from the waters of the Mississippi River.		
5	The government did not help at the beginning because of lack of money.		
6	Howard Leyland thought the worst thing about the situation was the lack of food and water.		
7	The government paid more than $60 billion to help the victims.		

PREPARATION: Writing an essay (for/against)

Read the instructions carefully. Brainstorm the pros and cons of the Internet in education.

Write your ideas under two headings:

Pros   Cons

Organise your ideas into a paragraph plan before you start to write. Put the pros and cons into separate paragraphs.

TIPS

- Use a fairly formal style. Avoid colloquial language.
- Use linking words to connect your ideas across sentences and paragraphs.
- You can write arguments on both sides of the question, but don't forget to give your own opinion in a clear conclusion.

EXAM TASK – Writing

Write an essay (120–180 words) for or against the following statement:

The Internet is a very important tool in education.

PREPARATION: Speaking

- Read the instructions. Who are you going to talk to and what about?
- Look at the Functions Bank on pages 101 for useful phrases on giving opinions and agreeing/disagreeing.

TIPS

- Think about what you have heard or read about the topic.
- Think about your own experience of the topic/situation to help you.
- Develop your arguments so that you have a full discussion of the topic. Express agreement and/or disagreement with your partner's ideas.
- Play the role you have been given, even if it is not really what you think; try to understand the other point of view and persuade your partner.

EXAM TASK – Speaking

You are talking to a friend from abroad about shopping. He/She is a fan of small shops, but you prefer supermarkets. Use these ideas for your dialogue:

Student A (in favour of supermarkets):

- Express your opinion on shopping in supermarkets.
- Mention the lower prices of goods and wider choice of products in supermarkets.
- Talk about other advantages (large parking spaces, convenient opening hours, etc.)

You can talk about your own ideas as well.

Student B (against supermarkets):

- Express your opinion on shopping in supermarkets.
- Criticise the quality of food in supermarkets.
- Talk about the advantages of smaller shops (friendly atmosphere, better for the environment, etc.)

You can talk about your own ideas as well.

9 Crime scene

A VOCABULARY AND LISTENING
Crimes and criminals

I can describe different crimes.

1 Complete the crossword puzzle.

1 Some _____ have damaged the computer – now it doesn't work.
2 He forgot to pay for the CDs, and when he got outside, a police officer arrested him for _____.
3 The _____ got into the house through an open window.
4 There was a _____ at the bank on the High Street this morning.
5 Don't leave money on your desk – there's a _____ in the building.
6 At night, _____ race cars up and down the street.
7 Somebody _____ my camera when I was at the beach.
8 The _____ went to prison for 25 years for killing his neighbour.

2 Complete the text with the verbs in the box.

committed   rob   sprayed   sold   stole   went
vandalised

According to newspaper reports, Liam Mason ¹_____ several crimes that night. First, he ²_____ a car and ³_____ joyriding in it. Then he ⁴_____ graffiti on an advertisement in town and ⁵_____ a bus stop. Then he ⁶_____ drugs to a 30-year-old man and tried to ⁷_____ a young woman. The woman was really a police officer and arrested him.

●●●●● **Extension:** Word formation: noun suffixes *-er*, *-ist*, and *-ian*

3 Look at the pictures. Complete the nouns with the correct suffix.

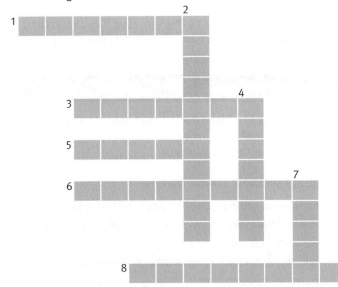

1 an art *ist*
2 a politic____
3 a sing____
4 a violin____
5 a photograph____
6 a novel____

4 Complete the sentences with nouns from exercise 3.

1 Paintings by the _____ Pablo Picasso are worth millions.
2 Nigel Kennedy is a famous _____ who has played with orchestras all over the world.
3 Bono is the _____ with the band U2.
4 Richard Avedon was a _____ who took pictures of famous people.
5 The _____ Joseph Conrad wrote in English.
6 Arnold Schwarzenegger used to be an actor but became a _____ .

Extra Practice

9B GRAMMAR
Past perfect

I can describe an event using different past tenses.

1 Look at the list of times and actions. Then write sentences using the past perfect, positive or negative.

LUCY – yesterday morning

7.15 – got up	8.35 – caught the bus
7.30 – had a shower	8.55 – arrived at school
8.00 – had breakfast	9.00 – began classes
8.15 – phoned Sarah	11.15 – finished homework during break
8.20 – left home	
8.30 – arrived at the bus stop	

1 When Lucy had breakfast, she <u>hadn't phoned</u> (phone) Sarah.
2 When Lucy had breakfast, she _____ (have) a shower.
3 At 8.32, Lucy _____ (arrive) at the bus stop.
4 At 8.45, Lucy _____ (arrive) at school.
5 At 9.10, Lucy _____ (begin) classes.
6 When Lucy began classes, she _____ (finish) her homework.

2 Write sentences about yourself at 8.30 yesterday morning. Use the past perfect, positive or negative.

By 8.30 in the morning …
1 (wake up) <u>I had woken up</u>
2 (get up) _____
3 (have breakfast) _____
4 (speak to a friend) _____
5 (watch TV) _____
6 (use my mobile) _____

3 Complete the sentences. Use the past simple for one gap and the past perfect for the other.

1 When I <u>got</u> (get) home, burglars <u>had stolen</u> (steal) my bike.
2 I _____ (look) out of the window; somebody _____ (spray) graffiti on our car.
3 Everybody _____ (leave) by the time I _____ (arrive) at the party.
4 I _____ (not have) any pizza because my brother _____ (eat) it.
5 My uncle _____ (look) different: he _____ (grow) a beard.
6 The robbers _____ (take) my friend's mobile phone, so he _____ (borrow) mine.

4 Put the verbs into the correct tense, past simple or past perfect.

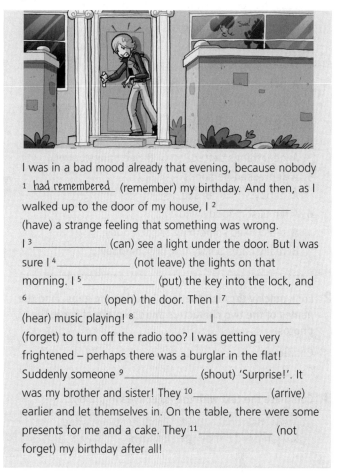

I was in a bad mood already that evening, because nobody ¹ <u>had remembered</u> (remember) my birthday. And then, as I walked up to the door of my house, I ² _____ (have) a strange feeling that something was wrong. I ³ _____ (can) see a light under the door. But I was sure I ⁴ _____ (not leave) the lights on that morning. I ⁵ _____ (put) the key into the lock, and ⁶ _____ (open) the door. Then I ⁷ _____ (hear) music playing! ⁸ _____ I _____ (forget) to turn off the radio too? I was getting very frightened – perhaps there was a burglar in the flat! Suddenly someone ⁹ _____ (shout) 'Surprise!'. It was my brother and sister! They ¹⁰ _____ (arrive) earlier and let themselves in. On the table, there were some presents for me and a cake. They ¹¹ _____ (not forget) my birthday after all!

●●●●●● CHALLENGE! ●●●●●●

Tick (✓) the things you had done before you were eight years old. Then write true sentences. Add four more ideas: two positive and two negative.

1 use a computer ☐   4 study English ☐
2 visit the USA ☐   5 watch a horror film ☐
3 learn to swim ☐   6 cook dinner for my family ☐

When I was eight, I had used / hadn't used a computer.
1 _____
2 _____
3 _____
4 _____
5 _____
6 _____
7 _____
8 _____
9 _____
10 _____

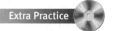

CULTURE

Inspector Morse

I can understand a story about a fictional character.

Revision: Student's Book page 86

1 Choose the correct endings for the definitions.

1 A **fictional** character exists in
   A stories, not real life. ☐   B real life, not stories. ☐

2 A **detective** is a kind of
   A police officer. ☐   B criminal. ☐

3 A **deerstalker** is a kind of
   A coat. ☐   B hat. ☐

4 A **magnifying glass** helps you to
   A hear things better. ☐   B see things better. ☐

5 A **depressed** person is
   A happy. ☐   B sad. ☐

6 A **fan** is somebody who
   A really likes something or somebody. ☐
   B really hates something or somebody. ☐

2 Look quickly through the text, ignoring the gaps. Find the names of the two characters and the make of car in the photos.

Characters: _____

Car: _____

3 Complete the text with the adjectives in the box.

> bored   fictional   final   intelligent   married
> old-fashioned   free   well-known

MORSE Inspector Morse is a famous
¹_____ detective. He is
the creation of the novelist Colin Dexter. Dexter studied at
Cambridge University and then worked as a teacher. He
started to write detective stories in his ²_____ time.
Today, Morse is ³_____ around the world because of
the TV programmes as well as the novels.

Morse works for the police. He lives in Oxford and drives a
large, ⁴_____ Jaguar car. He is an extremely
⁵_____ man and a very successful detective.
However, he is also a lonely and rather sad man who is easily
⁶_____ with everyday life. He is not ⁷_____
and his closest friend is Sergeant Lewis, a police officer who
works with him.

There are thirteen novels about Endeavour Morse. (Like
Sherlock Holmes, Morse has an extremely unusual first name!)
In the ⁸_____ novel, Morse dies. His fans were very
upset, but unlike Conan Doyle, author of the Sherlock Holmes
stories, Colin Dexter has refused to bring his hero back to life.

4 Read the statements about Sherlock Holmes. Tick (✓) the ones which are also true for Morse. Rewrite the ones which are not.

1 Holmes is a fictional detective. ✓

2 Holmes works for himself. ✗
   Morse works for the police.

3 Holmes is a rather sad man. ☐
   _____

4 Holmes' closest friend is a doctor. ☐
   _____

5 Holmes is not married. ☐
   _____

6 There are 25 stories about Holmes. ☐
   _____

7 Holmes has an extremely unusual first name. ☐
   _____

8 Holmes dies, but the author brought him back to life. ☐
   _____

●●●●●● **CHALLENGE!** ●●●●●●

Do you know any other famous fictional detectives (in films, TV, or books)? If so, add information about them to the chart.

Name of character	Writer	Titles of books/films	Character
Miss Marple	Agatha Christie	The Murder at the Vicarage	quiet, intelligent, determined

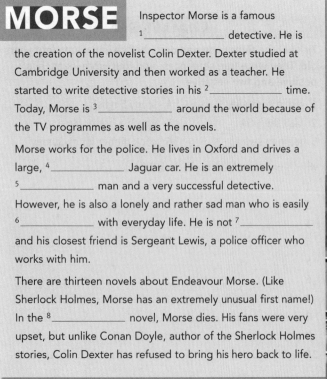

GRAMMAR
Reported speech

I can report what other people have said.

1 Complete the reported speech using the past simple or past continuous. Change the pronoun if necessary.

1 'I'm feeling ill,' he said.
 He said that *he was feeling ill.*

2 'It's raining,' she said.
 She said that _____

3 'I don't speak Japanese,' he said.
 He said that _____

4 'We don't eat meat,' they said.
 They said that _____

5 'It's very cold outside,' she said.
 She said that _____

6 'Drug dealers are criminals,' he said.
 He said that _____

7 'I live near the sea,' she said.
 She said that _____

8 'We're playing really well,' they said.
 They said that _____

9 'I'm not wearing a coat,' he said.
 He said that _____

2 Change the direct speech to reported speech. Use the past perfect. Change the pronoun if necessary.

Thieves stole my shoes!

You forgot to pay for the CDs.

1 He said that thieves had stolen his shoes.

2 _____

We bought lots of new clothes.

I didn't commit the robbery.

3 _____

4 _____

3 Read the dialogue. Then rewrite it as reported speech below.

Alan I'm looking for a detective story.

Mary I love detective stories. Inspector Morse is my favourite.

Alan I prefer Sherlock Holmes. He's a more interesting character.

Mary I read a Sherlock Holmes story recently. I didn't enjoy it.

Alan I'm not talking about the books, I'm talking about the films.

Mary I agree. The films are fantastic.

CRIME

Alan said that he was looking for a detective story .
Mary said that _____ .
She said that _____ .
Alan said that _____ .
He said that _____ .
Mary said that _____ .
She said that _____ .
Alan said that _____ .
He said that _____ .
Mary agreed. She said that _____ .

4 Read the reported speech. Then write the dialogue.

Juliet said that she didn't like Manchester. She said that she was lonely. Mark said that he knew a good café in Manchester. He said that it had great food and fantastic music. Juliet said that she couldn't go to the café because she didn't have any friends. She said that she hated going to cafés alone. Mark said that he had a friend in Manchester. He said that she was really nice. Juliet said that she wanted to meet her. Mark said that he was trying to find her phone number!

Juliet I don't like _____. I'm _____
_____.

Mark I know a _____. It has
_____.

Juliet I can't _____ because
_____. I hate
_____.

Mark I've got _____. She
_____.

Juliet I _____ her.

Mark I _____ number!

9E READING
Computer virus

I can understand an article about a crime.

Revision: Student's Book page 88

1 Match the pairs of adjectives with similar meanings. Which ones are more extreme? Complete the chart.

~~astonished~~ bad big brilliant clever delighted
enormous good happy important scared
small ~~surprised~~ terrible terrific terrified
tiny vital

adjective	extreme adjective
surprised	astonished

2 Match the two halves of the expressions.

1 to offer	**a** your guilt
2 to receive	**b** with a crime
3 to commit	**c** a reward
4 to admit	**d** a suspended sentence
5 to create	**e** a computer virus
6 to be charged	**f** a crime

3 Complete the text with the words in the box.

computer systems   crash   crime   damage   guilt
software   virus

'I love you'

On 3rd May 2000, millions of people around the world received an e-mail called 'I love you'. The e-mail included a document called 'Love letter for you'. When people opened this document, a ¹_____ destroyed hundreds of vital documents on their computer. The virus then sent a copy of itself to everybody in the e-mail address book. The virus infected millions of ²_____ across the world. Even computers in the White House in the USA were affected by the ³_____. The virus eventually caused about 10 billion dollars of ⁴_____.

4 Choose the best answers.

1 What did the virus do to people's computers?
   A It destroyed their e-mail address book. ☐
   B It sent them a love letter. ☐
   C It destroyed hundreds of vital documents. ☐

2 The virus infected
   A computer systems around the world. ☐
   B computer systems in the USA and Britain. ☐
   C computers in the Philippines. ☐

3 People think Onel de Guzman created the virus because
   A he has admitted it. ☐
   B it came from his computer. ☐
   C he was charged with computer crime. ☐

4 In the Philippines, laws against computer crime
   A did not exist in May 2000. ☐
   B do not exist now. ☐
   C have always existed. ☐

5 In the future, Onel de Guzman wants to
   A write software for governments and companies. ☐
   B write software for mobile phones and small computers. ☐
   C create more viruses. ☐

The person who created the virus was probably a brilliant 23-year-old computer student from the Philippines called Onel de Guzman. He has never admitted his ⁵_____, but detectives know that the virus came from his computer. Onel de Guzman was not charged with any ⁶_____ because in May 2000 the Philippines did not have any laws against computer crime. (They have now!)

Onel de Guzman did not finish his studies at computer school. He now lives with his sister and spends his time watching TV, reading books about computers and playing video games. In the future he wants to write more ⁷_____ – but this time, only games for mobile phones and hand-held computers. Governments and companies around the world will be delighted!

84 Unit 9 • Crime scene

9F

EVERYDAY ENGLISH

Reporting a theft

I can report a theft and describe what was stolen.

1 Match the lost property with the words in the box.

bus pass   credit card   keys   make-up   mobile phone
notepad   schoolbag   ~~traveller's cheques~~   wallet

 1
 2
 3
 4
 5
 6
 7
 8
 9

1   traveller's cheques
2   _____
3   _____
4   _____
5   _____
6   _____
7   _____
8   _____
9   _____

2 Order the words to make indirect questions.

1   Direct: What did you buy?
    Indirect: you / tell / bought? / Can / what / me / you
    Can you tell me what you bought?

2   Direct: Where's your brother?
    Indirect: is? / Have / idea / where / you / any / idea / brother / your
    _____

3   Direct: Is your friend at home?
    Indirect: you / home? / know / Do / at / your / if / friend / is
    _____

4   Direct: Where did you lose your bag?
    Indirect: you / bag? / lost / idea / Have / any / you / where / your
    _____

5   Direct: Is she an artist?
    Indirect: if / she's / Do / artist? / know / you / an
    _____

6   Direct: Who vandalised this bus?
    Indirect: bus? / tell / who / vandalised / you / Can / me / this
    _____

3 Rewrite these direct questions as indirect questions.

1   Who stole your bag?
    Have you any idea who stole your bag?

2   Is vandalism a problem here?
    _____

3   Where's the police station?
    _____

4   Is this your friend's wallet?
    _____

5   Why is your brother angry?
    _____

6   When did you leave home?
    _____

7   Does he live near here?
    _____

8   How often do you come into town?
    _____

4 Imagine you have lost something. Complete the chart. Choose from the ideas in the box or invent your own.

a wallet   a bag   a jacket   at the bus stop   2 hours ago
at the train station   yesterday   5 minutes ago
black   blue   brown   canvas   denim   leather
keys   cash   a credit card   some traveller's cheques

item lost	where and when?	colour	material	contents

5 Complete the dialogue. Rewrite the officer's questions as indirect questions. Write answers using the chart from exercise 4.

Officer   Good morning. How can I help?
You   I think somebody has stolen my _____
Officer   (Where and when did you last have it?)
             Have you any idea _____
You   I think I left it _____
Officer   (What colour is it?)
             Can you tell me _____
You   Yes, it's _____
Officer   (What is it made of?)
             Do you know _____
You   Yes. _____
Officer   (Is there anything inside it?)
             Do you know _____
You   Yes. _____
Officer   OK. Could you fill in this form, please?

Extra Practice

I can write a story describing a crime.

Preparation

1 **What tense are these verbs?**

1 didn't break, saw, arrived _____
2 were running, were looking, was walking _____
3 had phoned, had gone _____

2 Use the verbs in exercise 1 to complete the story.

Daylight robbery

As I ¹_____ home this evening, I ²_____ two boys outside a shop. They ³_____ in the shop window at the TVs and DVD players. Suddenly, one of them picked up a stone and threw it at the window. The window ⁴_____ but it made a lot of noise. After a while, the shopkeeper came out of the shop and shouted at them to stop, but they just laughed. Then he went back into the shop. As soon as he ⁵_____, the boys started throwing stones again, and this time they broke the window. They immediately took two DVD players and

3 **Read the story and put the pictures in the correct order.**

1 ☐   2 ☐   3 ☐   4 ☐   5 ☐   6 ☐

4 **Underline all the time expressions in the story.**

5 **Complete the sentences with the words in the box.**

earlier   end   following   one   soon   while

1 In the _____, the police caught the thieves.
2 After a _____, it started to rain.
3 _____ morning last week, I was playing football in the park.
4 A week _____, I had bought a new MP3 player.
5 The _____ day, I phoned my parents.
6 As _____ as I saw the thief, I phoned the police.

Writing task

6 **In your notebook write a story. Use the Writing Bank on page 104 to help you. Write 130–150 words and begin with these words:**

As I was walking home, I saw …

Check your work

Have you

☐ given your story a title?
☐ started the story correctly?
☐ used some time expressions?
☐ written 130–150 words?
☐ checked grammar, spelling and punctuation?

started to run away. But while he had been in the shop, the shopkeeper ⁶_____ the police. They ⁷_____ as the boys ⁸_____ across the road. The police officers jumped out of their car and arrested the boys.

Extra Practice

SELF CHECK 9

Read the clues and complete the crossword.

CLUES

Across (→)

2 When Julia got home, Harry _____ cooked dinner.

4 Oh, no! I think _____ has stolen my mobile phone!

6 She said that she _____ already seen the film.

10 'Is there any _____ in the bag?' 'Yes, my name and address are both in the bag.'

13 A _____ steals things from shops.

14 They said they _____ going to town.

16 The old lady said _____ she had seen the robbery.

17 He _____ three people so he's going to spend the rest of his life in prison.

19 'Hello. How can I _____ you?' 'I've lost my sports bag.'

20 The police caught the _____ when he tried to steal another car.

Down (↓)

1 A _____ visits places on holiday.

3 An _____ draws and paints pictures.

5 I was sure I _____ left my bag in the café.

7 'Can you _____ the wallet?' 'Yes. It's black and it's made of leather.'

8 Could you _____ in this form, please?'

9 Teenage boys often _____ this phone box. The phone never works.

11 J K Rowling is a _____.

12 Don't leave your wallet on the table. Somebody might _____ it.

15 A _____ builds houses.

18 Had you _____ your homework before you went to bed?

Your score ▮ /20

I CAN ...

Read the statements. Think about your progress and tick (✓) one of the boxes.

✳ = I need more practice. ✳✳ = I sometimes find this difficult. ✳✳✳ = No problem!

	✳	✳✳	✳✳✳
I can describe different crimes. (SB p.84)			
I can describe an event using different past tenses. (SB p.85)			
I can understand a story about a fictional character. (SB p.86)			
I can report what other people have said. (SB p.87)			
I can understand and react to an article about a crime. (SB p.88)			
I can describe and report something I have lost. (SB p.90)			
I can write a story describing a crime. (SB p.91)			

• • • • • • • • • • • • •

TIPS: Reading

- Read the text quickly to find out what it is about.
- Read the questions carefully.
- Then read the text again and identify which part of the text is relevant to each question.
- Decide if the information in the text is the same as or different from the information in the question.

EXAM TASK – Reading

Read the interview with a singer. Match the information in the statements (1–9) to the paragraphs (A–D). Then decide if the statements are true (T) or false (F).

A   You recently went to Greece to play with a band – how did that happen?

Shortly before I finished university, I got a call from a bass player living in Greece who wanted a singer for the summer. They were playing in a bar in a beautiful harbour town. He got my number from my singing teacher, who couldn't do it. He thought it would be a great opportunity for me to gain confidence and to sing somewhere else than in London bars. It was something I jumped at – a few days later I was on the plane. It was quite spontaneous!

B   Well, the best things usually are. Was singing away from London something you had always wanted to do?

To be honest, I'd never really thought about it before. It was perfect timing though, as I didn't have a clue what I was going to do after finishing my studies. It was a fantastic opportunity I couldn't miss. Plus, I can't say that I was sad to leave behind the smoky bars of London for a while! Since then, I've also played in Venice and toured around Italy and Germany. I think my time spent in Greece gave me the confidence to do this, though.

C   Well, I can believe that. How did you find the change of atmosphere – going from London bars to Greek ones?

It was great. Greece was breathtaking – beautiful mountains and flowers as far as the eye could see. The weather was great, too. It's much nicer spending evenings outside by the sea than in a smelly pub in the middle of London. I think the people were a bit more relaxed, too – not stressed by the fast city life like those I sing to at home. I also found the audiences more attentive in Greece, which did wonders for my confidence as a singer.

D   Did the time you spent away teach you anything else?

It taught me that I could go away from home on my own and be able to cope. I'd never been away from home for more than two weeks before and always with friends or family, so I grew up a lot while I was away. It was a positive experience in so many ways.

1 Before going to Greece, Kate had fixed plans for her future. _____
2 Kate enjoyed the atmosphere in Greece. _____
3 Her stay in Greece encouraged Kate to travel more. _____
4 Kate thought a lot about accepting the offer to go to Greece. _____
5 Thanks to her stay in Greece, Kate became more independent. _____
6 Kate was recommended to the band by a friend. _____
7 Kate was a little unhappy about leaving London. _____
8 People in Greece listened to Kate's songs carefully and with interest. _____
9 Kate was offered the job in Greece for one year. _____

• • • • • • • • • • • • •

TIPS: Listening

- Read the sentences carefully before you listen.
- The first time you listen, mark the statements that you think match the information in the recording. Check that you have the same number specified in the instructions.
- If necessary, find the missing answers when you listen again.

EXAM TASK – Listening

🎧 LISTENING 7   Listen to some information about the TV show *Lost*. Decide which four out of eight pieces of information are given in the recording.

A   More that 15.5 million people watched each episode of *Lost*. ☐
B   The series was based on a popular book. ☐
C   The pilot episodes of the show were very expensive. ☐
D   The story shows the lives of about 50 crash survivors on an island. ☐
E   The series is filmed on an island in the Caribbean. ☐
F   Fans of the show can watch it online. ☐
G   The show hasn't been very popular in Europe. ☐
H   You can buy books and magazines linked to the series. ☐

• • • • • • • • • • • • •

TIPS: Use of English

- Read the text to the end to find out what it is about.
- Try to fill in the missing words without looking at the options (A–D). This might help you to find the right answer.
- Read each sentence again carefully to check your answers.

Read the text about an interesting film. Some words are missing from the text. Choose the most appropriate option (A–D) for each gap (1–10) in the text.

William Shakespeare is probably the most famous playwright of all time. It is therefore quite surprising that little is ¹_____ about his life. There is a period between 1586 and 1592 ²_____ is a complete mystery even today. Was he a teacher in Wales, a travelling actor or perhaps a spy ³_____ these years? A new Spanish film, *Miguel and William*, may ⁴_____ another theory to the existing ones. The film-makers are suggesting that Shakespeare spent this time in Spain with Miguel Cervantes, author of the famous novel *Don Quixote*. And there seems to be some evidence for this. Both men ⁵_____ left their wives at that period and the film offers a romantic reason too – a Spanish actress ⁶_____ Leonor that both men are believed to be in love ⁷_____.The other interesting fact is the change of writing style in both ⁸_____ fiction. After 1592, Shakespeare started ⁹_____ tragedies and Cervantes created *Don Quixote*. Perhaps the ¹⁰_____ will never be known but the film gives us an entertaining look at the past.

1	A to know	B know	C knowing	D known
2	A that	B what	C it	D this
3	A for	B during	C while	D since
4	A adding	B adds	C add	D added
5	A had	B have	C has	D were
6	A call	B calling	C calls	D called
7	A for	B by	C with	D at
8	A man's	B men's	C man	D men
9	A writing	B wrote	C written	D write
10	A truth	B true	C right	D rights

PREPARATION: Writing a formal letter

Read the instructions and answer the following questions:

- What kind of letter should you write: formal or personal?
- What information do you need to include?
- How will you divide your letter into paragraphs?

Use the Writing Bank on page 102 to help you.

TIPS

- When you have finished, make sure you have included all the required information.
- Count the words and adjust the length, if necessary.

You have decided to apply for a summer job in Oxford. You have seen this advertisement in a local newspaper:

Hotel Blue Lagoon

offers seasonal work for students at the hotel reception.

We are looking for young people with knowledge of at least one foreign language.

Write an application letter (120–180 words) to the hotel manager, including the following points:

- basic information about yourself
- your education
- your skills
- a short personality description, taking the advertised job into consideration

PREPARATION: Speaking

1 Note down words and phrases for the following categories:

- types of music
  _____
- adjectives describing music
  _____
- people involved in making music
  _____

2 Remember phrases for talking about likes and dislikes, and making arrangements.

Use the Functions Bank on pages 100–1 to help you.

Task 1
You are planning to go to a music festival with a friend from Britain. Use these ideas for your dialogue. You may add your own ideas.

- Tell him/her what kind of music you like most, and why.
- Ask your friend about his/her favourite kind of music.
- Suggest a day and time to go to the festival.
- Agree together on the day to go to the festival and the concert to see.

Task 2
You have decided to buy tickets to see your favourite team play in a basketball match. Go to the stadium to buy two tickets (ask about price, front seats, and the possibility of taking pictures and/or recording the match). Use all these ideas for the role-play. You may add your own ideas.

A VOCABULARY AND LISTENING
Publications

I can identify and talk about different publications.

1 Solve the anagrams and write the publications.

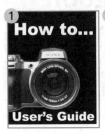   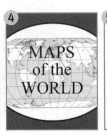   

  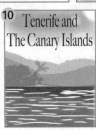 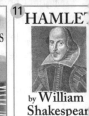

1 unlaam
  <u>manual</u>

2 hyootaubigrap
  _____

3 nvole
  _____

4 satla
  _____

5 repsenwap
  _____

6 btxtekoo
  _____

7 acyceniedloap
  _____

8 yekocor obko
  _____

9 arcindtoiy
  _____

10 koodigueb
  _____

11 alyp
  _____

12 agemanzi
  _____

13 mcoci
  _____

14 hygobirap
  _____

2 Complete the sentences with a publication from exercise 1.

1 I'm going to make something special for dinner. Can I borrow your <u>cookery book</u>?

2 I'm not sure what 'ignorant' means. I'm going to look in a _____.

3 I don't know how to programme my new DVD recorder. I should look in the _____.

4 I'm going to Madrid for the weekend. Can I borrow your _____?

5 We've got a chemistry lesson today and my _____ is at home.

6 I'm reading a fantastic _____. It's a thriller about a murderer.

7 Have you got today's _____? I want to find out what's on TV tonight.

8 I'm going to see a Shakespeare _____ at the theatre tomorrow evening.

●●●●● **Extension:** books and text

3 Look at the pictures. Answer the questions.

1 Is it a hardback or a paperback?
  _____

2 Where is the title printed?
  _____

3 What is printed on the spine?
  _____

4 Is it a hardback or a paperback?
  _____

5 What page is this?
  _____

 Extra Practice

GRAMMAR
The passive (present simple)

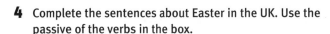
I can describe the different stages of a process.

1 Write the words in the correct order to make passive sentences.

1 This / printed / book / China / in / is
This book is printed in China.

2 made / Laws / by / Parliament / are
_____

3 year / committed / crimes / A / of / lot / are / every
_____

4 is / made / Cheese / milk / from
_____

5 played / in / Rugby / Australia / is
_____

6 all / world / the / Shakespeare's / performed / are / plays / over
_____

2 Complete the sentences about the making of a hotel guidebook. Use the passive, present simple.

1 First, hotels _are contacted_ (contact) by phone.
2 A lot of hotels _____ (visit).
3 Photographs _____ (take) of the rooms.
4 The best hotels _____ (choose).
5 A description _____ (write) of each hotel.
6 The photos and descriptions _____ (check) by an editor.
7 The book _____ (print).
8 The book _____ (sell) in bookshops and online.

3 Use the sentences in exercise 2 to order the pictures.

4 Complete the sentences about Easter in the UK. Use the passive of the verbs in the box.

give	roll	~~see~~	decorate	sell	hide

1 Eggs __are seen__ as symbols of the Easter holiday or springtime.
2 Chocolate eggs and decorated eggs _____ as gifts at Easter.
3 Chocolate eggs _____ in large numbers every year at Easter.
4 Real eggs _____ in different colours.
5 Small eggs _____ in the garden for children to find.
6 Sometimes real eggs _____ down a hill in a competition.

●●●●●● CHALLENGE! ●●●●●●

Write four sentences in the present passive about other special occasions. Use the ideas in the box to help you.

All Saints Day   Christmas   Halloween   Mother's Day
New Year's Eve   St Nicholas's Day   Twelfth Night
Valentine's Day

A twelve-course meal is eaten on Christmas Day.

1 _____
_____
2 _____
_____
3 _____
_____
4 _____
_____

Romeo and Juliet

I can understand information about a Shakespeare play.

Revision: Student's Book page 96

1 Match the two halves of the definitions.

1 A **playwright** is ☐
2 A **sonnet** is ☐
3 A **theatre** is ☐
4 To **retire** means ☐
5 To **get married** means ☐
6 To **be buried** means ☐
7 To **be christened** means ☐

a to be named at a special ceremony in church.
b a person who writes plays.
c to become somebody's husband / wife.
d a place where plays are performed.
e to be put under the ground when you are dead.
f a poem with 14 lines.
g to stop working.

2 Do you know the story of Romeo and Juliet? Number the pictures in the correct order.

 a ☐
 b ☐
 c ☐
 d ☐
 e ☐
 f ☐
 g ☐
 h ☐

3 Read the text and check your answers to exercise 2.

Romeo and Juliet

Romeo and Juliet by Shakespeare is probably the most famous love story in the world. It is about two teenagers in Verona, Italy – a boy and a girl – who meet and fall in love. Unfortunately, Romeo is a member of the Montague family and Juliet is from the Capulet family. The two families hate each other and often fight. If the parents knew about the love between Romeo and Juliet, they would stop them from seeing each other, so the two teenagers decide not to tell anybody. They get married at a secret ceremony. Only the priest , Friar Lawrence, is there.

The conflict between the two families continues and Romeo kills one of Juliet's cousins in a fight. He has to leave Verona and move to another city in Italy called Mantua.

Friar Lawrence wants Romeo and Juliet to be together. He gives Juliet a special potion that will make her sleep for two days and appear dead. Later, she will wake up, escape from her family in Verona and join Romeo in Mantua.

Juliet drinks the potion and appears to be dead, although she's only sleeping. However, Romeo doesn't know about the Friar's plan. He thinks Juliet really is dead. He is so upset that he drinks poison and dies. Later, Juliet wakes up, sees that Romeo is dead, and kills herself with Romeo's knife.

4 Complete the sentences with highlighted words from the text.

1 A _____ is a special drink that has magical powers.
2 _____ means fights and arguments.
3 _____ is something that kills you, or makes you ill, if you eat or drink it.
4 A _____ is somebody who leads people in their religion.
5 Your _____ are the children of your uncle / aunt.

●●●●● **CHALLENGE!** ●●●●●

Do the quiz about Shakespeare. Then check your answers by looking at the text on Student's Book page 96.

1 What was Shakespeare's first name?
   A William ☐   B Harry ☐   C Hamlet ☐
2 When was Shakespeare born?
   A 1564 ☐   B 1664 ☐   C 1764 ☐
3 What was the name of Shakespeare's wife?
   A Anne ☐   B Juliet ☐   C Judith ☐
4 Shakespeare wrote plays and also
   A novels ☐   B poems ☐   C a dictionary ☐
5 Shakespeare also worked as
   A an artist ☐   B an actor ☐   C a teacher ☐

1 Write sentences in the passive, past simple.

1 this book / write / in 1956
   This book was written in 1956.

2 this car / make / in Japan
   _____

3 *Lost in Translation* / direct / by Sofia Coppola
   _____

4 the pyramids / build / more than 4,500 years ago
   _____

5 the crime / commit / at five o'clock this morning
   _____

6 the photo / take / by my sister
   _____

2 Compare these two pictures of the same street. What has changed?

1 rubbish / pick up
   The rubbish has been picked up.

2 bus stop / repair
   _____

3 flowers / plant
   _____

4 pavement / clean
   _____

5 hedge / cut
   _____

6 house / sell
   _____

3 Choose the correct tense in these passive sentences.

1 The book **was** / **has been** published 5 years ago.
2 Since then, it **was** / **has been** read by millions of people.
3 Last year, it **was** / **has been** translated into Chinese.
4 A lot of newspaper articles **were** / **have been** written about the book since its publication.
5 It **was just** / **has just been** made into a film.

4 Complete the text. Use the passive form of the verbs in brackets, past simple or present perfect.

The Queen of Crime

Agatha Christie is the most popular novelist in history. She was born in 1890 in the south of England. Christie didn't go to school. She ¹ _was educated_ (educate) at home by her mother.

She started writing while she was working as a nurse in the First World War. Her first book ² _____ (complete) in twelve months, but it ³ _____ (not publish) until 1920, five years later. Since then, over two billion of her books ⁴ _____ (sell). Two famous fictional detectives – Miss Marple and Hercule Poirot – ⁵ _____ (create) by Agatha Christie.

Her books ⁶ _____ (translate) into more than 100 languages, and in the 1960s and 70s several of her works ⁷ _____ (make) into films.

●●●●● CHALLENGE! ●●●●●

Find information about your favourite author. Answer these questions with full sentences.

1 Where was he / she educated?
   _____

2 When was his / her first book published?
   _____

3 How many of his / her books have been sold?
   _____

4 What book is he / she best know for?
   _____

5 Have his / her books been translated into other languages?
   _____

6 Have any of his / her books been made into films? (If yes, give an example.)
   _____

10 E
Philip Pullman

I can understand an interview with an author.

Revision: Student's Book page 98

1 Choose the best equivalent of these sentences.

1 He was educated at home.
  A He had school lessons at home.
  B He a difficult time at home.

2 Her first book became a best-seller.
  A A lot of people bought her first book.
  B Her first book was her best book.

3 He didn't intend to become a writer.
  A He didn't like being a writer.
  B He didn't plan to become a writer.

4 She likes crime stories as long as they aren't violent.
  A She likes crime stories if they're long but not violent.
  B She likes crime stories but not violent ones.

5 She doesn't believe in telepathy.
  A She doesn't know what other people are thinking.
  B She doesn't think you can know what is in somebody else's mind.

6 He's very persistent.
  A He tries and tries again.
  B He understands everything.

7 She isn't very disciplined.
  A She isn't well-organised.
  B She isn't well-known.

8 He's a humble man.
  A He doesn't think he is too important.
  B He isn't very tall.

9 He doesn't like criticism.
  A He doesn't like hearing other people's opinions of his work.
  B He doesn't like working hard.

2 Read the article about Philip Pullman. Which sentence describes him best?

A An Australian writer of fantasy who likes watching *Neighbours* on television.

B A writer of fairy tales and comics who went to Oxford University.

C An English author who has written some famous fantasy novels.

Philip Pullman

Philip Pullman is a writer of fantasy. He was born in England but spent his early childhood travelling from country to country with his parents. While he was in Australia he started reading comics, and grew to love *Superman* and *Batman*. Later, the family moved back to England. Pullman studied English at Oxford University and then worked as a teacher. He eventually left his job to be a full-time writer. His most famous work is *His Dark Materials*, a trilogy of three novels.

Interviewer Why do you believe stories are so important?
Pullman Because they entertain and they teach; they help us both to enjoy life and endure it. After nourishment, shelter and companionship, stories are the thing we need most in the world.

Interviewer Where and when do you write?
Pullman I write in my shed, at the bottom of the garden. I write by hand, using a pen. I write three pages every day (one side of the paper only). That's about 1,100 words. Then I stop. After lunch, I always watch *Neighbours* on television. Soap operas are interesting.

Interviewer Which books have made a difference to you?
Pullman The books which have made the most difference to my life have been *Grimm's Fairy Tales*, Homer's *Iliad* and *Odyssey*, the *Sherlock Holmes* stories of Arthur Conan Doyle, and the *Superman* and *Batman* comics which were published when I was young.

3 Choose the best meaning for the highlighted words in the text.

1 eventually: **A** at first ☐ **B** finally ☐
2 a trilogy: **A** a set of three works ☐ **B** one large work ☐
3 to endure: **A** accept (something bad) ☐ **B** enjoy ☐
4 nourishment: **A** stories ☐ **B** food ☐
5 companionship: **A** life ☐ **B** friends ☐

4 Write the questions for these answers.

1 When did he start reading comics?
  While he was in Australia.

2 _____
  At Oxford University.

3 _____
  Because they teach and entertain.

4 _____
  In his shed.

5 _____
  About 1,100 words.

0F EVERYDAY ENGLISH
Buying books

I can ask for information in a bookshop.

1 Put these ten books in the ten correct bookshop departments. Then think of a book for the other five departments (English or your own language).

1 adult fiction _____
2 art _____
3 biography _____
4 children's fiction _____
5 cookery _____
6 health and fitness _____
7 history _____
8 humour _____
9 languages _____
10 nature _____
11 poetry and drama _____
12 reference _____
13 science and technology _____
14 sport _____
15 travel _____

2 Order the words to make sentences. Then match them to the meanings (a–e).

1 in/ have / stock. / We / don't / it
   We don't have it in stock. _____

2 it / shelves. / can't / on / the / see / I
   _____

3 take? / it / long / will / How
   _____

4 help / I / if / you / wonder / me. / could
   _____

5 for / it / you. / order / can / I
   _____

a When will it arrive? ☐
b I can arrange for it to be sent here. ☐
c We haven't got it in the shop. ☐
d Could you help me, please? ☐
e I can't find it. ☐

3 Complete the dialogue using the sentences (1–5) from exercise 2.

Jenny Hello. 1 _____.
I'm looking for *Eragon* by Christopher Paolini.

Assistant It'll be in the adult fiction section.

Jenny 2 _____.

Assistant I'll look on the computer. No, I'm sorry,
3 _____.
4 _____.

Jenny 5 _____?

Assistant Only two or three days.

Jenny OK. That's fine.

4 Write another dialogue. Use one of the books from exercise 1 and this information.

- the book isn't in stock
- the assistant can order it
- it will take 10 days to arrive
- you can't wait that long

Mark Hello. I wonder _____.
I'm looking _____.

Assistant It'll be in _____.

Mark I can't _____.

Assistant I'll look _____. No,
I'm sorry, _____.
I can _____.

Mark How _____?

Assistant _____.

Mark No, sorry. _____.

A book review

I can write a review of a book.

Preparation

1 Read the review and complete the information about the book that Suzie recommends.

Title	Eragon
Author	
Type of book	
Set in ...	
Main character	
What happens?	

2 Match the two halves of the sentences.

1	I identified with	**a**	a robot and a young girl.
2	I liked the book because	**b**	it's a really gripping story.
3	In the end	**c**	at the end.
4	It was written by	**d**	an author called Dan Brown.
5	It's a	**e**	a film.
6	It's set in	**f**	the main character.
7	It's the story of	**g**	Joanna Simpson, a young English woman.
8	It was made into	**h**	science fiction story.
9	The main character is	**i**	London in the 25th century.
10	There's a twist	**j**	the main character dies.

3 Complete the sentences with a style of fiction from the box.

> classic novels   comic novels   crime   fantasy
> historical novels   ~~horror~~   science fiction   short stories

1 ___Horror___ books are scary and often violent.
2 _____ books are often set in the future.
3 _____ are always set in the past.
4 _____ books are set in an imaginary world and often include magic.
5 _____ are funny.
6 _____ are written by great authors from the past.
7 _____ are not as long as novels.
8 _____ stories are often about detectives.

A book review   *by Suzie*

I've just read a really good book. It's called *Eragon* and it was written by Christopher Paolini. It's the first in a trilogy of fantasy novels and it's set in an imaginary place called Alagaësia. It was recently made into a really good film.

It's the story of a 15-year-old boy who finds a strange blue stone in the mountains. It's actually a dragon's egg! He and the dragon become friends. It's the start of an adventure full of magic, wars and death. There's a twist at the end, but I won't give it away.

I liked the book because the author has created an amazing fantasy world. It contains a lot of interesting characters and I really wanted to know what was going to happen. I thoroughly recommend it.

Writing task

4 In your notebook write a review of a book you liked or didn't like. Use the Writing Bank on page 104 to help you. Write 130–150 words. Follow this plan:

Paragraph 1
Title, author, type of book
Paragraph 2
Characters and story
Paragraph 3
Why you liked / didn't like it

> **Check your work**
>
> **Have you**
> ☐ divided your review into three paragraphs?
> ☐ used some phrases from exercise 2?
> ☐ written 130–150 words?
> ☐ checked spelling, punctuation and grammar?

THE #1 NEW YORK TIMES BESTSELLER

ERAGON
Christopher Paolini

SELF CHECK (10)

Read the clues and complete the crossword.

CLUES

Across (→)

1. I _____ if you could help me. I'm looking for a book on trees.
4. These are _____ letters: ABCDE.
6. Can I pay _____ credit card?
7. I'm looking for a Spanish–English _____ .
9. _____ computers used in your school?
10. An _____ is a book of maps of all the countries in the world.
12. A lot of tea _____ grown in India.
13. Bananas _____ grown in England.
14. There's a _____ between these words: hitch-hike.
15. *Romeo and Juliet* was _____ by William Shakespeare.
18. I never read the _____ . I watch the news on TV instead.

Down (↓)

2. I'm sorry. We've sold _____ of that book.
3. Is this book paperback or _____ ?
5. Tina is reading a fashion _____ .
6. The character of Sherlock Holmes was created _____ Arthur Conan Doyle.
8. We don't have that book in stock, but I can _____ it for you.
11. You can find books about planets and stars in the _____ and technology section.
15. The first *Harry Potter* book _____ published in 1997.
16. The _____ of this book is *Maturita Solutions Workbook*.
17. Shakespeare's plays have _____ translated into hundreds of languages.

Your score ___ /20

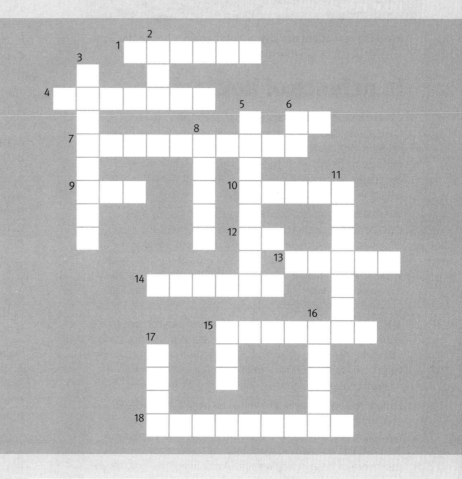

I CAN ...

Read the statements. Think about your progress and tick (✓) one of the boxes.

✳ = I need more practice.   ✳✳ = I sometimes find this difficult.   ✳✳✳ = No problem!

	✳	✳✳	✳✳✳
I can identify and talk about different publications. (SB p.94)			
I can describe the different stages of a process. (SB p.95)			
I can understand information and opinions on Shakespeare. (SB p.96)			
I can use different forms of the passive. (SB p.97)			
I can understand an interview with an author. (SB p.98)			
I can ask for information in a bookshop. (SB p.100)			
I can write a review of a book. (SB p.101)			

EXAM TASK – Reading

Read the text about the city of Nottingham. Choose the best answer (A–D) to the questions (1–6).

In defence of Nottingham

The newspapers call Nottingham 'the capital of crime', and there are statistics that seem to prove it: 115 crimes per 1,000 residents, 5.2 murders per 100,000 residents, four times as much crime as the worst parts of London. In fact, a recent newspaper report says Nottingham is the most dangerous city in Britain. But a local writer, Tom Bates, likes his city.

So what is Nottingham like? In many parts of the city there is clearly evidence of crime – you can hear police cars and ambulances, there are teenagers in hooded tops hanging around. However, Tom lives his life without coming into contact with crime. Tom has never seen a gun on the streets – not even the police carry guns – and the last time he noticed a boy in a hoodie, he was helping an old lady.

In fact, Tom likes his neighbourhood a lot. He lives in a small, busy area of red-brick houses. He has access to many shops and cafés and there's a large park nearby. The shops and facilities are within easy walking distance from his house, and Tom often meets friends and neighbours when he is out running errands.

So Tom decided to speak to some of his neighbours to see if their experience of Nottingham reflected the articles in the newspaper. He spoke to some teachers, and asked them about the latest crime headlines. 'Well, they don't reflect my experience of living in Nottingham,' Alexis Jones told him. 'It's an image that's been created by the media.' Alexis has never felt that he is in danger in the city. The violence is limited to criminal gangs and it is easy to be safe.

Next, Tom spoke to Mr and Mrs Xiao, who work in his community. Mr Xiao was mugged some time ago, and their house was burgled. They want to move to a new town.

Isabelle Sanders, a mother with a young baby, is thinking about moving away from the city too. Her brother was mugged in Nottingham. But she says 'It's not just the crime, it's air pollution, traffic, things like that.' She doesn't think Nottingham is worse than other cities.

Tom started to realise that everyone he spoke to had a story about crime. It seemed Nottingham is dangerous, but he is still not convinced by the idea that it is the most dangerous city in Britain. Everyone he spoke to agreed about one thing: all big cities are dangerous.

There are lots of positive aspects of Nottingham. People know each other, and there is a sense of community. In fact, people want to live in Nottingham. It is a city that is small enough to walk around. It has pleasant parks and green spaces. The city centre is busy and energetic and there is an active cultural scene with new art, music and writing. Tom thinks the newspapers have been too negative. He feels that Nottingham is a pleasant place, a community that has been unfairly called 'the capital of crime'.

1 The article's aim is to
   A show how dangerous Nottingham is.
   B react to the newspaper stories about Nottingham.
   C present the good sides of Nottingham.
   D describe life in Nottingham.

2 The author is aware of crime in the city because
   A he was attacked by a boy in a hooded top.
   B he saw an elderly lady robbed on a bus.
   C there are groups of suspicious-looking youths.
   D there are armed police everywhere.

3 Tom describes his neighbourhood as
   A friendly and comfortable.
   B friendly but without any amenities.
   C overpopulated and unfriendly.
   D dangerous and full of violence.

4 The first people Tom spoke to said that
   A Nottingham is a city of gang culture.
   B violence has been exaggerated by the media.
   C Nottingham was fairly presented by the media.
   D Nottingham is a city without any violence.

5 Isabelle Sanders is going to move away because
   A of the inconveniences of a big city.
   B of crime and violence.
   C of her newborn baby.
   D her brother was mugged.

6 The conclusion of the article is that Nottingham
   A has more armed criminals than other cities.
   B has got all the inconveniences of a big city.
   C has more advantages than disadvantages.
   D is an artistic city.

EXAM TASK – Use of English

Complete the text with the correct form of the words in brackets (1–11).

People usually see graffiti as vandalism. On the other hand, some see ¹_____ (hide) messages, and believe graffiti is ²_____ (person) and ³_____ (meaning), and maybe even beautiful. In my work I deal with my life and the lives of others who live on the street. My paintings reflect the ⁴_____ (real) of the world I live in.

Graffiti is art although it may be in the wrong place at times. I would like to bring it to a higher level. I want my paintings to be not only on walls, but also on clothing, in magazines and in ⁵_____ (advertise).

I have been influenced by many artists and ⁶_____ (write). But I do not have any models. All graffiti artists keep their names ⁷_____ (know) or use their 'tag' so no one really knows who they are.

To me, graffiti is a mural on the side of a ⁸_____ (build). Graffiti is a slogan found in a bathroom. Graffiti is a political or ⁹_____ (art) logo on a post office box or traffic sign. Graffiti is in your face. Graffiti is ¹⁰_____ (legal). Graffiti is ¹¹_____ (danger). Graffiti is ART.

TIPS: Listening

- Read the text and decide what kind of information you need to listen for.
- Listen to the recording and fill in as many gaps as you can. Use the words from the recording.
- Listen again and complete the rest of the text. Check the words you have already written.

EXAM TASK – Listening

🎧 LISTENING 8 Listen to the interview with a writer called Mary Colville. Complete the missing information in the text.

Mary Colville has written ¹_____ _____ books for adults and children. She started writing when she was ²_____ years old, and her first novel was written at the age of ³_____. In recent years, Mary has been writing ⁴_____ for television dramas. She wrote short stories for magazines in the ⁵_____. At the moment she is writing the ⁶_____ part of *The Secrets of the Night*. She relaxes at home with the books of Yann Martel and Jane Austen, and she is also a ⁷_____ _____ of Philip Pullman's books.

PREPARATION: Writing a story

- Set the scene – who, where, what, when – in the introduction.
- Put the events in chronological order (including the ending).
- In the conclusion, you may want to describe the feelings of the main character.
- Use linkers to sequence the story.

Use the Writing Bank on page 104 to help you.

EXAM TASK – Writing

Write a story (120–180 words), starting with these words:

Peter suddenly woke up in the middle of the night.

Include the following points in your story:

- the scene and the characters
- what happened
- the feelings of the people involved and your feelings

TIPS: Speaking

- Think of words and phrases to describe each photo.
- Make a list of similarities and differences. Think of both the reason and effect of what the people are doing.
- When answering questions, think about *Who / What / When / Why / How?*

EXAM TASK – Speaking

1 Compare the photos about environmental issues.
   - What are the similarities/differences in the pictures? (where, what, how, why, etc.)
   - Which picture do you prefer, and why?

2 Answer these questions.
   - Do you have/Would you like to have a recycling programme at your school?
   - What do you personally do to help the environment?
   - What should people in your country do to help the environment?

Picture 1

Picture 2

FUNCTIONS BANK

STARTING A CONVERSATION

Hello. My name's (David). What's your name?

Where are you from?

Pleased to meet you.

How are you?

I'm fine, thanks.

How are things?

What are your hobbies?

Do you do any sports?

Have you got any brothers or sisters?

Where do you live?

Which school do you go to?

TALKING ABOUT LIKES AND DISLIKES

What do you like doing in your free time? (1F)

What else do you like doing?(1F)

Who's your favourite (singer)?(1F)

What's your favourite (food)? (1F)

How much time do you spend (watching TV)? (1C)

I love (surfing the Internet). (1F)

I enjoy (going to the cinema). (1F)

I can't stand (playing football). (1F)

I hate (shopping). (1F)

(Tennis) is OK. (1F)

I prefer (watching TV). (1F)

REACTING TO WHAT THE OTHER PERSON SAYS

Me too. (1F)

So do I. (1F)

Really? (1F)

That's interesting. (1F)

Do you? (1F)

Cool. (2F)

What about you? (2F)

GIVING DIRECTIONS

Where's (the sports centre)? (3F)

Is there (a bank) near here? (3F)

Can you tell me how to get there? (3F)

It's opposite / next to etc. (the bank). (3F)

It's on the corner. (3F)

Go straight on. (3F)

Go past (the sports centre). (3F)

Turn (right) into (Kings Rd). (3F)

Turn (left) at (the traffic lights). (3F)

Go along (Kings Rd). (3F)

Take the (first) (right). (3F)

Go to the end of the road. (3F)

SHOPPING

Good (morning). Can I help? (4F)

The (jeans) are over there. (5F)

What size are you? (5F)

We don't have it in stock, but I can order it for you. (10F)

I'm afraid we've sold out of (that book). (10F)

That's (£50), please. (5F)

Here's your change. (4F)

Here you are. (4F)

Can I have your card number, please? (4F)

Good morning. I wonder if you could help me. (10F)

I'm looking for (a jumper). (5F)

I'd like (a pair of jeans), please. (4F)

Have you got it in (blue)? (5F)

Have you got it in a (12)? (5F)

Can I try (it) on? (5F)

It doesn't fit very well. (5F)

How much is it? (5A)

Can I pay by credit card? (10F)

OK. I'll take it. (5A)

Can I bring it back (if it doesn't fit)? (5F)

ARRANGEMENTS

What are you up to? (6F)

Nothing much. (6F)

Do you fancy meeting up later? (6F)

Why don't we meet (at the cinema)? (6F)

Where do you want to meet? (6F)

Where are we going to meet exactly? (6F)

What time? (6F)

See you later. (6F)

I'll see you at (two o'clock). (6F)

OK. Great! (6F)

CHECKING UNDERSTANDING

Pardon? (4F)

Sorry. Did you say ...? (4F)

Could you repeat that, please? (4F)

INVITATIONS

What are your plans for the weekend? (7F)

I'm having a party tomorrow. Would you like to come? (7F)

Do you fancy (going out this evening)? (1F)

Do you fancy joining us? (7F)

Why don't you come along? (7F)

Sorry you can't make it. (7F)

That's a shame. (7F)

Glad you can make it. (7F)

Great. See you there. (7F)

Sure. Good idea. (1F)

That sounds great. (7F)

I'll definitely be there. (7F)

I'd love to, thanks. (7F)

I'm sorry, I can't. (7F)

Sorry, but I won't be able to make it. (7F)

What time? (7F)

Shall I bring (some food)? (7F)

See you tomorrow. (7F)

GIVING ADVICE

Can I ask your advice about something? (8F)

OK, thanks. That's a good idea. (8F)

Sure. What's the problem? (8F)

I think you should ... (8F)

I think you ought to ... (8F)

I don't think you should ... (8F)

In my opinion, you shouldn't ... (8F)

If I were you, I'd ... (8F)

Why don't you ...? (8F)

DESCRIBING PICTURES

I can see ...

In the background ...

In the foreground ...

On the right ...

On the left ...

I'm not sure what that is.

I'm not sure what (he's doing).

I think ...

I don't think ...

GIVING OPINIONS

I think ...

I don't think ...

In my opinion ...

On the other hand ...

That's true, but ...

I agree.

I don't agree.

What do you think of ...?

What's ... like?

What do you think?

Do you agree?

WRITING BANK

Informal letters

- Start the letter with *Dear* and the person's first name.
- We sometimes start a letter by asking how the person is.
- Divide the letter into short paragraphs, each with its own topic.
- We can use colloquial words and phrases.
- We can end the letter with an expression like *Write soon*, *Best wishes*, or *Take care*, and your first name. If we know the person well, we can use *Love*, *Lots of love* or *With love from*.
- Use P.S. to add extra information or ask a question at the end of the letter.

Dear Clare,

How are things? It was great to see you during the holidays and thanks for showing me all the sights of York. I had a fantastic time.

I started university here in Prague last week. There's so much information and so many new people to meet. I think the course is going to be really interesting and I'm sure I'll have a lot of fun here.

How is your new job? Are you enjoying it? It must be really nice to be earning some money. I'm going to try to get a part-time job while I'm studying here. A bit of extra cash will be really useful. There's a bookshop in the city centre that's advertising for staff so I might go there and have a chat with them.

Well, I've got to get back to the books. Write soon.

Best wishes,
Kuba

P.S. Are you going to come and visit me next year?

Formal letters

Dear Sir or Madam,

I am writing to apply for the holiday job in your restaurant, which I saw advertised in the Evening News last week.

I am seventeen years old, a student at Newton's College, and have lots of experience working in restaurants and cafés. Last summer I worked as a waiter in Mario's Café and recently I have been working at The Bay Leaf in High Street. I am hard-working, honest and have good customer service skills.

I would be grateful if you could send me some more details about the job and I would be happy to discuss my application with you. I am enclosing my CV.

I look forward to hearing from you.

Yours faithfully,

Tina White

- Start the letter with *Dear* and the person's title and family name. Use *Mr* for men, *Mrs* for married women and *Miss* for single women.
- If we don't the know the name of the person we are writing to, we start the letter *Dear Sir or Madam*.
- In the first paragraph, we usually say why we are writing.
- In the next paragraph, we write the important information.
- To ask for something we can use set phrases such as *Could you please …*, or *I would be grateful if you could … .*
- If we want a reply, we can write *I look forward to hearing from you.* after the final paragraph.
- Do not use colloquial language or short forms, e.g. *I'm*, *you're*.
- We finish the letter with *Yours sincerely* if we used the person's name at the start, or *Yours faithfully* if we didn't. We write our whole name.

Notes: accepting or declining an invitation

- Start the note with *Dear* or *Hi* and the person's name.
- Finish the note with *Love* or *Best* wishes and your name.
- We often use abbreviations when we write notes.
- We don't usually divide the text into paragraphs.
- We can use colloquial words and phrases.

Dear Simon,

I got your note. Great to hear from you. Thanks very much for the invitation to the barbecue in your garden. I'd love to come. I'm really looking forward to it.

Love
Samantha

P.S. Do you want me to bring anything? I've got loads of good party music.

A leaflet

- Include an eye-catching title and slogans.

- Use bullet points.

- Use short informative sentences.

- You can address the reader directly.

- You can include contact details, if appropriate.

Action on Homelessness

- There are over 500 homeless people in our city.
  - Many of them are under 20 years old.

How would you feel if you didn't have a home and had to sleep on the streets?

LET'S DO SOMETHING ABOUT IT!

DAY OF ACTION: 4th May

We are collecting warm clothes to give to homeless people. If you have any old clothes that you don't need, please bring them to the school hall.

For more information ring Harriet on
562265

'The differences between boys and girls are natural and are present when a child is born.' Do you agree?

This is an issue on which people hold strong views. Some people argue that male and female brains are different and that this causes differences in behaviour. However, I believe that most of the differences are the result of the way in which we bring up children at home and at school.

At home, most parents give toy cars and guns to their sons and dolls to the daughters. In my view, this encourages boys to be aggressive and girls to be caring and sensitive.

Furthermore, at school more boys do science and maths than girls. In my opinion, this is not because boys are naturally better at these subjects but because there are more male scientists, who act as role models.

In conclusion, I believe that boys and girls are born the same, and that the way we treat them as children makes them different from each other.

An opinion essay

- Start with a general statement.

- Give your opinion in the first paragraph.

- Put each argument or example in a separate paragraph.

- Use set phrases to express your opinions.

- Use linking words to join phrases and sentences.

- In the conclusion, summarise your argument and give your opinion again.

A review

- Give the title and type of book or film and other relevant background information.

- Divide your review into paragraphs.

- Summarise the story, but don't give away the ending.

- Mention both things you liked and things you didn't like.

- Give your overall opinion in the final paragraph.

Spiderman 3 is the latest in the highly popular Spiderman series. It's a science-fiction adventure starring Tobey Maguire.

The character of Spiderman is based on the superhero of the comic book stories. Peter Parker is a teenager who gains supernatural powers when a spider bites him. In this film we see a darker side to his character as he fights the evil Sandman and Venom.

As in the other Spiderman films, the special effects are amazing, especially in the fight scenes. The soundtrack too is excellent, with songs by Snow Patrol and Burning Lips. However, I wasn't impressed with either the acting or the story. I thought Tobey Maguire was very unconvincing and the story was very predictable.

Overall I enjoyed the film, although personally I wouldn't go and see it again. Having said that, fans of Spiderman movies won't be disappointed.

Last summer my girlfriend Jane and I were outside Buckingham Palace, taking photos. It was a lovely sunny day. I took a photo of Jane and then she took one of me.

I was just putting my camera away when a tall, young man approached us and kindly offered to take a photo of the two of us together, with Buckingham Palace in the background. So I showed him how to use the camera and we stood in front of the railings. I thought it was a bit strange because he kept walking backwards, much further than I thought was necessary. Then, suddenly, he turned round and ran off with my camera! I shouted but he kept on running.

Luckily for us, there was a police officer not far away and he saw what had happened and caught the thief.

A story

- We usually use the past tense in stories or narratives.

- The first paragraph usually sets the scene (who, where, when, what).

- Divide your story into paragraphs.

- Give a definite ending to your story.

- Use time expressions.

- Add background detail.

- Use adjectives and write about your feelings.

- Use adverbs to make your story interesting.

- Use linking words to join phrases and sentences.

1 Complete the text with appropriate words.

Paula Radcliffe is ¹_____ British long-distance runner. She ²_____ born in the north of England in 1973, and by the age of 20 was competing ³_____ world championships. However, she did not start running marathons until ten years later. She was immediately successful, and won the London marathon ⁴_____ 2002. The following year, she not only won the London marathon, but ⁵_____ set a new world record for the women's marathon with a time of 2 hours, 15 ⁶_____ and 25 seconds.

Because ⁷_____ her success, many people expected Paula Radcliffe to win the marathon at the Olympic Games in Athens in 2004, but she had to stop after 36 kilometres. Five days later, she took ⁸_____ in the 10,000 metres, but again was unable to finish the race. This was a low point in Paula's career ⁹_____ an athlete, and some people thought it was the beginning of the end, but they were wrong. She won marathons in New York and London in 2005, making her ¹⁰_____ of the most successful runners in the history of athletics.

Mark /10

2 Choose the correct words to complete the magazine article.

What is an au pair?

An au pair is a young person age 17–27, often a student, who lives with a family in a foreign country for six months or a year. Au pairs are there to practise the language and learn about the culture of the host country. They ¹ help / helps to look after the children and do housework, and in return they become like a member of the family. They ² eat / are eating with the family and take part in family life. They also receive some money for their work: £55 a week is the legal minimum for 25 hours' work.

A personal experience

Eleven months ago, Renata ³ comes / came to London as an au pair from Poland. ⁴ She lives / She's living with a British family until the end of next month. Here are some of her thoughts about her time in England.

"I decided ⁵ to become / becoming an au pair because I wanted to improve my English. I ⁶ am / was / were very nervous when I ⁷ meet / meeted / met the family for the first time at Heathrow Airport, but they were so ⁸ friendly / mean / rude that I soon felt OK. The children weren't ⁹ shy / confident / friendly at all – they started chatting to me immediately.

The family live in ¹⁰ a quite / quite a / the quiet big house, and I have my own room. In the evenings, I spend time ¹¹ to watch / watching TV with the family. I work 30 hours a week, but I don't work at weekends. On Saturdays, I play ¹² gymnastics / volleyball at the sports centre, and on Sundays I ¹³ sometimes go / go sometimes shopping. While I ¹⁴ came / was coming home from the shops a few weeks ago, I met another au pair from Poland on the bus. She ¹⁵ didn't like / wasn't liking her family at all. I suppose I was lucky with mine!"

Mark /15

TOTAL /25

1 Complete the second sentence so that it means the same as the first. Include the word in brackets.

1 *Spiderman 3* is shorter than *Pirates of the Caribbean*.
Spiderman 3 _____ as *Pirates of the Caribbean*. (LONG)

2 Life in a small village is usually quite relaxing.
Life in a small village _____ stressful. (VERY)

3 Old houses are rare in this town.
There _____ in this town. (MANY)

4 I didn't meet many interesting people on holiday.
I only _____ interesting people on holiday. (FEW)

5 In my opinion, no actress is more attractive than Keira Knightley.
In my opinion, Keira Knightley _____ world. (MOST)

6 Rural areas in Scotland are not very polluted.
There _____ rural areas in Scotland. (POLLUTION)

7 It's too cold to have lunch outside.
It _____ to have lunch outside. (WARM)

8 My brother isn't old enough to watch horror films.
My brother _____ to watch horror films. (TOO)

9 Now we've finished our exams, shall we go to the cinema?
Now we've finished our exams, _____ to the cinema? (DON'T)

10 They need more money to finish making the film.
They _____ finish making the film. (ENOUGH)

Mark /10

Arial 10 **A** **B** *I* U

Hi Joel

How are you? Everything is fine here. We ¹ had / were having exams at school last week. They were ² more easy / easier than last year, but I didn't do ³ revision enough / enough revision . I'm not as hard-working ⁴ as / than you!

Did I ⁵ told / tell you about Joanna? She's the new au pair for the family next door. I ⁶ was meeting / met her for the first time while she was playing ⁷ gymnastics / volleyball / cycling with the children in the garden. I saw her again on Saturday morning and I invited her to the cinema to see the new Tarantino film. I was really ⁸ exciting / excited about the evening, but it all went wrong. First, Joanna got lost in town. And then, when she finally arrived at the cinema, she ⁹ didn't can / couldn't buy a ticket because she's ¹⁰ too young / young too . (It's an 18 certificate.)

¹¹ We go / We're going on holiday next week to a village in the countryside. We know ¹² a / the village because we went there last year. It's really small. There are only ¹³ a few / a little cottages and there aren't ¹⁴ some / any shops or busy roads. But the scenery is beautiful, and there's a ¹⁵ hedge / pavement / stream next to the cottage with really clean water.

E-mail soon!

Dan

Mark /15

TOTAL /25

1 Complete the article with the correct form of the verbs in the box.

> admit be be buy cost have learn receive
> reveal waste

More than one in five electronic gadgets are never used because people are frightened of new technology, a survey has ¹_____. Britons ²_____ £1.25 billion a year giving friends and relatives unwanted gadgets as gifts. Everything from iPods to sat-navs are still sitting in their boxes. The research by Scooter Computer magazine shows that, on average, the unwanted gadgets ³_____ £120. Apple's iPod ⁴_____ the most common unwanted gift, followed by digital cameras, computer software, sat-navs and mobile phones. The survey shows that people aged 35 to 44 ⁵_____ the worst for leaving gadgets unused. Will Foot, of Scooter Computer magazine, said: 'Many people just do not ⁶_____ the time to ⁷_____ how their gift works and others are scared of change.'

Jan Sorensen, 47, of Putney, South-West London, was very disappointed when she ⁸_____ digital photo software at Christmas. She had been given a digital camera a month earlier – and it was still in its box. She ⁹_____: 'I got a refund and ¹⁰_____ some clothes. I am scared of new technology.'

Mark ▢ /10

2 Choose the correct words to complete Oliver's thank-you letter.

Dear Uncle Simon,

Thank you so much for the DVDs you sent me for my birthday. I ¹ have watched / watched 'The Incredibles' yesterday with Ellie. I ² loved / was loving it! It's one of the ³ better / best / worst films I've ever seen. I haven't watched the other two films ⁴ already / yet .

I got ⁵ some / any great presents. Mum and Dad gave me a ⁶ calculator / camcorder / stereo , so I can listen to music in my room. In fact, ⁷ I listen / I'm listening to a CD now.

Joanna gave me a pen. If you press a secret button on it, the pen ⁸ will become / becomes a radio. It's really cool. Ellie didn't ⁹ bought / buy me a present this year because she hasn't got ¹⁰ much / many money. I don't mind not ¹¹ to get / getting a present from her, she's only five.

On my birthday, we all went to the Sea Life Centre in Brighton. It was really interesting. We saw ¹² much / a lot of different animals but the ¹³ most / more exciting were the sharks. Have you ¹⁴ already / ever seen a shark? They've got really scary eyes.

That's all for now. ¹⁵ I'm going to / I'll watch one of the other DVDs this afternoon. Thanks again!

Love,

Oliver

Mark ▢ /15

TOTAL ▢ /25

1 Complete the text with the correct word: A, B, C or D.

In the UK ¹_____, people throw away about 1,500 kg of food packaging ²_____ second. It makes up about 25% of household waste. This is a ³_____ problem for the environment, and it is also expensive. The amount of rubbish that ordinary families produce is increasing by 3% every year. The ⁴_____ of collecting this rubbish is about £2.5 billion, and rising.

Where does all this packaging go? A lot of it ends up ⁵_____ China. Each year, the UK ⁶_____ China to receive about two million tonnes of its waste. Most of the plastic waste goes to Lianjiao, a small village in the south of the country. As a result, the river there has become dirty and the air is ⁷_____. There is also a growing problem with ⁸_____, as some of the workers at the recycling centres are as young as four.

Most people agree that the companies who make sandwiches, pizzas and other products should take action. If they used less packaging, it ⁹_____ reduce the amount of waste. So some newspapers and politicians in the UK are telling people that they ¹⁰_____ to take unnecessary plastic packaging back to the supermarket and leave it there.

	A	B	C	D
1	one	lonely	alone	single
2	all	any	ever	every
3	big	strong	heavy	bad
4	money	cost	price	refund
5	at	upon	on	in
6	affords	costs	earns	pays
7	polluted	stressful	busy	noisy
8	homelessness	famine	child labour	racism
9	can	must	will	would
10	should	ought	must	mustn't

Mark ___ /10

2 Choose the correct words to complete the chat room page.

Hi everybody! I'm an Italian au pair in Tackley. It's ¹ **a** / **the** small village near Oxford. There's nothing to do here. It's so ² **boring** / **gripping** / **impatient** . Help!
Paola from Italy

Hi Paola. Are there any hills near your village? You should ³ **play** / **do** / **go** cycling.
Nuria from Spain

The weather isn't ⁴ **very good** / **enough good** / **good enough** to go cycling. It's cold and wet most days. I ⁵ **usually stay** / **am staying** / **stay usually** at home and watch DVDs. I like funny films. Does anybody know any good comedies?
Paola from Italy

Hi, Paola. Try the new Jennifer Aniston film. It isn't her ⁶ **funnier** / **funniest** , but it's ⁷ **more** / **most** entertaining than The Break-up.
Alexa from Hungary

You're lucky, Paola. I wish ⁸ **I live** / **I lived** / **I'd live** in Tackley. I live in London and I hate it. There's a lot of poverty and homelessness. If I had the choice, ⁹ **I** / **I'd** / **I'll** live in a small village in the countryside.
Nuria from Spain

Next weekend, ¹⁰ **I'm going to** / **I'll** visit London for the first time. Do you want to meet up, Nuria? If you give me your number, ¹¹ **I'll phone** / **I phone** / **I phoned** you.
Paola from Italy

I live in London too. There are ¹² **the** / **some** / **any** beautiful parks in the centre. I think Hyde Park is the nicest. We should all meet there.
Alexa from Hungary

OK. ¹³ **I don't know** / **I'm not knowing** my mobile number at the moment. It's just changed and I haven't learned it ¹⁴ **already** / **yet** . Give me your numbers. ¹⁵ **I'll** / **I'm going to** call you soon, I promise.
Nuria from Spain

Mark ___ /15

TOTAL ___ /25

1 Complete the text with the words in the box.

become	crime	guilty	history	minutes	sell
sentence	stolen	thieves	trial		

Stephen Blumberg and His Stolen Books

In an unusual case, Stephen C. Blumberg was today given a six-year prison ¹_____ for the theft of rare books from libraries and universities. At his ²_____, he was found ³_____ of stealing more than 20,000 books from 327 different places. In total, the books were worth about $20 million, making this the largest ⁴_____ of its kind in American ⁵_____.

Like many book ⁶_____, Blumberg was also a book lover. According to a friend, he didn't go to bed at night but instead read books until morning, falling asleep in his chair for a few ⁷_____ at a time, then waking up to continue reading. He did not ⁸_____ any of the books that he had ⁹_____, but stored them tidily in his 17-room home in Ottumwa, Iowa. His ambition, according to his friend, was to ¹⁰_____ the greatest rare-book thief of the century.

Mark ___ /10

2 Choose the correct words to complete Joanna's blog.

Hi everyone!

Thanks for reading my blog. I'm sorry that ¹ I'm not writing / I don't write / I haven't written anything for weeks - I've been really busy. Finally, I've got ² a little / a few time on my own with the computer! Ellie and Oliver have ³ been / gone to bed, and Jim and Sarah ⁴ watch / are watching a film in the other room.

It was Daniel's birthday last Sunday and ⁵ he's had / he had a barbecue. I didn't know it was his birthday, so I ⁶ haven't / hadn't bought a present for him. (I bought him a book the next day.) The barbecue was good fun. I met ⁷ some / any really interesting people. But the ⁸ most / best / more exciting part was the badminton tournament. I won it! While we were in the garden, some wallets ⁹ was / were stolen from the house. Daniel called the police, but they ¹⁰ weren't coming / didn't come.

This is my last month in England. ¹¹ I'll go / I'm going home in three weeks! I wish I ¹² can / could stay a bit longer, but I've already bought my plane ticket. I phoned the travel agency, but they said that I ¹³ didn't / couldn't change it. I've really enjoyed ¹⁴ living / to live with this family. I'm sure I'll see them again soon. If I have enough money, ¹⁵ I'm visiting / I'll visit / I'd visit them next year.

Mark ___ /15

TOTAL ___ /25

WORDLIST

This list contains the key words from the units in the Student's Book.

Word	Phonetics	Translation
Unit 1 The real you		
addicted (adj)	/əˈdɪktɪd/	....
agree (v)	/əˈgriː/	....
allow (v)	/əˈlaʊ/	....
ambitious (adj)	/æmˈbɪʃəs/	....
attractive (adj)	/əˈtræktɪv/	....
avoid (v)	/əˈvɔɪd/	....
baggy (adj)	/ˈbægi/	....
ban (v)	/bæn/	....
behave (v)	/bɪˈheɪv/	....
believable (adj)	/bɪˈliːvəbl/	....
certain (adj)	/ˈsɜːtn/	....
chess (n)	/tʃes/	....
comfortable (adj)	/ˈkʌmftəbl/	....
confident (adj)	/ˈkɒnfɪdənt/	....
cool (adj)	/kuːl/	....
decide (v)	/dɪˈsaɪd/	....
fancy (v)	/ˈfænsi/	....
fat (adj)	/fæt/	....
fearless (adj)	/ˈfɪələs/	....
fit (adj)	/fɪt/	....
for sale (adj)	/fə ˈseɪl/	....
friendly (adj)	/ˈfrendli/	....
funny (adj)	/ˈfʌni/	....
generation gap (n)	/dʒenəˈreɪʃn ˌgæp/	....
generous (adj)	/ˈdʒenərəs/	....
grateful (adj)	/ˈgreɪtfl/	....
hard-working (adj)	/ˌhɑːdˈwɜːkɪŋ/	....
hide (v)	/haɪd/	....
hooded top (n)	/ˈhʊdɪd ˌtɒp/	....
hoodie (n)	/ˈhʊdi/	....
hope (v)	/həʊp/	....
imagine (v)	/ɪˈmædʒɪn/	....
impatient (adj)	/ɪmˈpeɪʃnt/	....
intolerant (adj)	/ɪnˈtɒlərənt/	....
judge (v)	/dʒʌdʒ/	....
karate (n)	/kəˈrɑːti/	....
keen ('I'm keen on') (adj)	/kiːn/	....
kind (adj)	/kaɪnd/	....

Word	Phonetics	Translation
lazy (adj)	/ˈleɪzi/	....
leisure (adj)	/ˈleʒə(r)/	....
loyal (adj)	/ˈlɔɪəl/	....
mean (adj)	/miːn/	....
mind ('I don't mind') (v)	/maɪnd/	....
online (adv)	/ɒnˈlaɪn/	....
optimistic (adj)	/ɒptɪˈmɪstɪk/	....
pal (n)	/pæl/	....
patient (adj)	/ˈpeɪʃnt/	....
pessimistic (adj)	/pesɪˈmɪstɪk/	....
phobic (adj)	/ˈfəʊbɪk/	....
photography (n)	/fəˈtɒgrəfi/	....
polite (adj)	/pəˈlaɪt/	....
politician (n)	/pɒləˈtɪʃn/	....
pretend (v)	/prɪˈtend/	....
punk (n)	/pʌŋk/	....
quiet (adj)	/ˈkwaɪət/	....
refuse (v)	/rɪˈfjuːz/	....
rude (adj)	/ruːd/	....
serious (adj)	/ˈsɪəriəs/	....
shy (adj)	/ʃaɪ/	....
silly (adj)	/ˈsɪli/	....
stand ('I can't stand') (v)	/stænd/	....
stupid (adj)	/ˈstjuːpɪd/	....
support (v)	/səˈpɔːt/	....
talkative (adj)	/ˈtɔːkətɪv/	....
terrible (adj)	/ˈterəbl/	....
tolerant (adj)	/ˈtɒlərənt/	....
trendy (adj)	/ˈtrendi/	....
trouble-maker (n)	/ˈtrʌblmeɪkə(r)/	....
unfair (adj)	/ʌnˈfeə(r)/	....
unfriendly (adj)	/ʌnˈfrendli/	....
unkind (adj)	/ʌnˈkaɪnd/	....
wedding (n)	/ˈwedɪŋ/	....

Get ready for your exam 1

Word	Phonetics	Translation
background (n)	/ˈbækgraʊnd/	....
foreground (n)	/ˈfɔːgraʊnd/	....

WORDLIST

Word	Phonetics	Translation
Unit 2 Winning and losing		
accident (n)	/ˈæksɪdənt/	....
achievement (n)	/əˈtʃiːvmənt/	....
amazing (adj)	/əˈmeɪzɪŋ/	....
athletics (n)	/æθˈletɪks/	....
attack (v)	/əˈtæk/	....
badminton (n)	/ˈbædmɪntən/	....
bank (of a river) (n)	/bæŋk/	....
baseball (n)	/ˈbeɪsbɔːl/	....
basketball (n)	/ˈbɑːskɪtbɔːl/	....
bench (n)	/bentʃ/	....
bite (v)	/baɪt/	....
blood (n)	/blʌd/	....
boat (n)	/bəʊt/	....
building (n)	/ˈbɪldɪŋ/	....
catch fire (v)	/ˌkætʃ ˈfaɪə(r)/	....
cheat (v)	/tʃiːt/	....
cheer (n)	/tʃɪə(r)/	....
cheer (v)	/tʃɪə(r)/	....
clear (adj)	/klɪə(r)/	....
come back (v)	/ˌkʌm ˈbæk/	....
compete (v)	/kəmˈpiːt/	....
compete in (v)	/kəmˈpiːt ɪn/	....
competition (n)	/ˌkɒmpəˈtɪʃn/	....
cox (n)	/kɒks/	....
crash (v)	/kræʃ/	....
cycling (n)	/ˈsaɪklɪŋ/	....
discrimination (n)	/dɪˌskrɪmɪˈneɪʃn/	....
event (n)	/ɪˈvent/	....
eventually (adv)	/ɪˈventʃuəli/	....
experience (n)	/ɪkˈspɪəriəns/	....
fall over (v)	/ˌfɔːl ˈəʊvə(r)/	....
football (n)	/ˈfʊtbɔːl/	....
freestyle (n)	/ˈfriːstaɪl/	....
game (n)	/ɡeɪm/	....
go away (for the weekend) (v)	/ˌɡəʊ əˈweɪ/	....
goal (n)	/ɡəʊl/	....
golf (n)	/ɡɒlf/	....
gymnastics (n)	/dʒɪmˈnæstɪks/	....
hang (v)	/hæŋ/	....
hit (v)	/hɪt/	....
huge (adj)	/hjuːdʒ/	....
hurdles (n)	/ˈhɜːdlz/	....
ice hockey (n)	/ˈaɪs ˌhɒki/	....
immediately (adv)	/ɪˈmiːdiətli/	....
incredible (adj)	/ɪnˈkredəbl/	....
joke (v)	/dʒəʊk/	....
judo (n)	/ˈdʒuːdəʊ/	....
karate (n)	/kəˈrɑːti/	....
kick (v)	/kɪk/	....
lead (v)	/liːd/	....
lift (give someone a lift in your car) (n)	/lɪft/	....
lose (v)	/luːz/	....
lose control (v)	/ˌluːz kənˈtrəʊl/	....
medal (n)	/ˈmedl/	....
oar (n)	/ɔː(r)/	....
pass (a ball) (v)	/pɑːs/	....
penalty (n)	/ˈpenəlti/	....
pitch (n)	/pɪtʃ/	....
point (n)	/pɔɪnt/	....
professional (adj)	/prəˈfeʃnl/	....
race (n)	/reɪs/	....
racket (n)	/ˈrækɪt/	....
referee (n)	/refəˈriː/	....
relay (n)	/ˈriːleɪ/	....
river (n)	/ˈrɪvə(r)/	....
row (v)	/rəʊ/	....
rower (n)	/ˈrəʊə(r)/	....
rugby (n)	/ˈrʌɡbi/	....
score (v)	/skɔː(r)/	....
scream (v)	/skriːm/	....
send off (v)	/send ˈɒf/	....
shake (v)	/ʃeɪk/	....
shot (play a tennis shot) (n)	/ʃɒt/	....
shout (v)	/ʃaʊt/	....
sink (v)	/sɪŋk/	....

WORDLIST

Word	Phonetics	Translation
spare time (n)	/ˌspeə ˈtaɪm/	....
spectator (n)	/spekˈteɪtə(r)/	....
sponsor (n)	/ˈspɒnsə(r)/	....
sprint (n)	/sprɪnt/	....
steer (v)	/stɪə(r)/	....
success (n)	/səkˈses/	....
superior (adj)	/suːˈpɪəriə(r)/	....
surfing (n)	/ˈsɜːfɪŋ/	....
swimming (n)	/ˈswɪmɪŋ/	....
table tennis (n)	/ˈteɪbl ˌtenɪs/	....
talented (adj)	/ˈtæləntɪd/	....
tennis (n)	/ˈtenɪs/	....
throw (v)	/θrəʊ/	....
volleyball (n)	/ˈvɒlibɔːl/	....
wave (v)	/weɪv/	....
weightlifting (n)	/ˈweɪtlɪftɪŋ/	....
win (v)	/wɪn/	....
world champion (n)	/ˌwɜːld ˈtʃæmpiən/	....
yard (n)	/jɑːd/	....

Unit 3 Town and country

Word	Phonetics	Translation
across (prep)	/əˈkrɒs/	....
advertisement (n)	/ədˈvɜːtɪsmənt/	....
along (prep)	/əˈlɒŋ/	....
ancient (adj)	/ˈeɪnʃnt/	....
atmospheric (adj)	/ˌætməsˈferɪk/	....
basketball (n)	/ˈbɑːskɪtbɔːl/	....
behind (prep)	/bɪˈhaɪnd/	....
between (prep)	/bɪˈtwiːn/	....
computer game (n)	/kəmˈpjuːtə ˌgeɪm/	....
cottage (n)	/ˈkɒtɪdʒ/	....
dust (n)	/dʌst/	....
empty (adj)	/ˈempti/	....
enormous (adj)	/ɪˈnɔːməs/	....
extraordinary (adj)	/ɪkˈstrɔːdnri/	....
famous (adj)	/ˈfeɪməs/	....
farm (n)	/fɑːm/	....
fascinating (adj)	/ˈfæsɪneɪtɪŋ/	....
field (n)	/fiːld/	....

Word	Phonetics	Translation
footpath (n)	/ˈfʊtpɑːθ/	....
gate (n)	/geɪt/	....
head teacher (n)	/ˌhed ˈtiːtʃə(r)/	....
hedge (n)	/hedʒ/	....
hill (n)	/hɪl/	....
historic (adj)	/hɪˈstɒrɪk/	....
homework (n)	/ˈhəʊmwɜːk/	....
industrial (adj)	/ɪnˈdʌstriəl/	....
industry (n)	/ˈɪndəstri/	....
inhabitant (n)	/ɪnˈhæbɪtənt/	....
lane (n)	/leɪn/	....
librarian (n)	/laɪˈbreəriən/	....
lonely (adj)	/ˈləʊnli/	....
near (prep)	/nɪə(r)/	....
next to (prep)	/ˈnekst tu, ˈnekst tə/	....
on the corner of (prep)	/ɒn ðə ˈkɔːnərəv/	....
opposite (prep)	/ˈɒpəzɪt/	....
over (prep)	/ˈəʊvə(r)/	....
past (prep)	/pɑːst/	....
pavement (n)	/ˈpeɪvmənt/	....
peaceful (adj)	/ˈpiːsfl/	....
pedestrian crossing (n)	/pəˈdestriən/	....
polluted (adj)	/pəˈluːtɪd/	....
pollution (n)	/pəˈluːʃn/	....
pop music (n)	/ˈpɒp mjuːzɪk/	....
population (n)	/pɒpjəˈleɪʃn/	....
postbox (n)	/ˈpəʊstbɒks/	....
road sign (n)	/ˈrəʊd saɪn/	....
roadworks (n)	/ˈrəʊdwɜːks/	....
rubbish bin (n)	/ˈrʌbɪʃ ˌbɪn/	....
rural (adj)	/ˈrʊərəl/	....
scenery (n)	/ˈsiːnəri/	....
shopping centre (n)	/ˈʃɒpɪŋ ˌsentə(r)/	....
sight (n)	/saɪt/	....
silent (adj)	/ˈsaɪlənt/	....
situated (adj)	/ˈsɪtʃueɪtɪd/	....
spectacular (adj)	/spekˈtækjələ(r)/	....
state (n)	/steɪt/	....
stream (n)	/striːm/	....

WORDLIST

Word	Phonetics	Translation
street lamp (n)	/'stri:t læmp/	....
stressful (adj)	/'stresfl/	....
stunning (adj)	/'stʌnɪŋ/	....
sweatshirt (n)	/'swetʃɜ:t/	....
swimming pool (n)	/'swɪmɪŋ ˌpu:l/	....
table tennis (n)	/'teɪbl ˌtenɪs/	....
through (prep)	/θru:/	....
tiny (adj)	/'taɪni/	....
traffic jam (n)	/'træfɪk ˌdʒæm/	....
traffic lights (n)	/'træfɪk ˌlaɪts/	....
treasurer (n)	/'treʒərə(r)/	....
urban (adj)	/'ɜ:bn/	....
valley (n)	/'væli/	....
vast (adj)	/vɑ:st/	....
village (n)	/'vɪlɪdʒ/	....
weekend (n)	/'wi:kend, wi:k'end/	....
wonderful (adj)	/'wʌndəfl/	....
wood (n)	/wʊd/	....

Get ready for your exam 3

Word	Phonetics	Translation
cheerleading (n)	/'tʃɪəli:dɪŋ/	....
cyclist	/'saɪklɪst/	....
disappointed (adj)	/dɪsə'pɔɪntɪd/	....
individual determination (n)	/ˌɪndɪ'vɪdʒuəl dɪˌtɜ:mɪ'neɪʃn/	....
lose (v)	/lu:z/	....
match (n)	/mætʃ/	....
players (n)	/'pleɪəz/	....
race (n)	/reɪs/	....
score (v)	/skɔ:(r)/	....
team spirit (n)	/ˌti:m 'spɪrɪt/	....
win (v)	/wɪn/	....

Get ready for your exam 4

Word	Phonetics	Translation
afford (v)	/ə'fɔ:d/	....
bright (adj)	/braɪt/	....
clean (adj)	/kli:n/	....
comfortable (adj)	/'kʌmftəbl/	....
cosy (adj)	/'kəʊzi/	....

Word	Phonetics	Translation
dark (adj)	/dɑ:k/	....
detached (adj)	/dɪ'tætʃt/	....
flatmate (n)	/'flætmeɪt/	....
furnished (adj)	/'fɜ:nɪʃt/	....
neighbourhood (n)	/'neɪbəhʊd/	....
relaxing (adj)	/rɪ'læksɪŋ/	....
rent (n)	/rent/	....
share (v)	/ʃeə(r)/	....
tidy (adj)	/'taɪdi/	....
tube station (n)	/'tju:b ˌsteɪʃn/	....
uncomfortable (adj)	/ʌn'kʌmftəbl/	....
untidy (adj)	/ʌn'taɪdi/	....

Unit 4 In the spotlight

Word	Phonetics	Translation
action film (n)	/'ækʃn ˌfɪlm/	....
affair (n)	/ə'feə(r)/	....
animated film (n)	/'ænɪmeɪtɪd ˌfɪlm/	....
annoying (adj)	/ə'nɔɪɪŋ/	....
award (n)	/ə'wɔ:d/	....
(be) based on (v)	/'beɪst ɒn/	....
book (v)	/bʊk/	....
boring (adj)	/'bɔ:rɪŋ/	....
charming (adj)	/'tʃɑ:mɪŋ/	....
classic (adj)	/'klæsɪk/	....
comedy (n)	/'kɒmədi/	....
confusing (adj)	/kən'fju:zɪŋ/	....
convincing (adj)	/kən'vɪnsɪŋ/	....
director (n)	/də'rektə(r)/	....
disappointing (adj)	/dɪsə'pɔɪntɪŋ/	....
disaster film (n)	/dɪ'zɑ:stə ˌfɪlm/	....
display (v)	/dɪ'spleɪ/	....
documentary (n)	/dɒkju'mentri/	....
drama (n)	/'drɑ:mə(r)/	....
embarrassing (adj)	/ɪm'bærəsɪŋ/	....
entertaining (adj)	/entə'teɪnɪŋ/	....
exhausting (adj)	/ɪg'zɔ:stɪŋ/	....
film industry (n)	/'fɪlm ˌɪndəstri/	....
frightening (adj)	/'fraɪtənɪŋ/	....
gripping (adj)	/'grɪpɪŋ/	....

WORDLIST

Word	Phonetics	Translation
historical drama (n)	/hɪ'stɒrɪkl ˌdrɑːmə(r)/	....
horror film (n)	/'hɒrə ˌfɪlm/	....
intelligence agent (n)	/ɪn'telɪdʒəns ˌeɪdʒənt/	....
interesting (adj)	/'ɪntrəstɪŋ/	....
moving (adj)	/'muːvɪŋ/	....
musical (n)	/'mjuːzɪkl/	....
(the) news (n)	/ðə 'njuːz/	....
OAP (old-age pensioner) (n)	/ˌəʊ eɪ 'piː/	....
overall (adj)	/ˌəʊver'ɔːl/	....
play (v)	/pleɪ/	....
reckless (adj)	/'rekləs/	....
romantic comedy (n)	/rəʊ'mæntɪk ˌkɒmədi/	....
scary (adj)	/'skeəri/	....
scene (n)	/siːn/	....
science fiction film (n)	/ˌsaɪəns 'fɪkʃn ˌfɪlm/	....
screenplay (n)	/'skriːnpleɪ/	....
sensitive (adj)	/'sensətɪv/	....
starring (adj)	/'stɑːrɪŋ/	....
surface (n)	/'sɜːfɪs/	....
surprising (adj)	/sə'praɪzɪŋ/	....
thriller (n)	/'θrɪlə(r)/	....
violent (adj)	/'vaɪələnt/	....
war film (n)	/'wɔː fɪlm/	....
western (n)	/'westən/	....

Unit 5 Gifts

Word	Phonetics	Translation
aspirin (n)	/'æsprɪn/	....
bakery (n)	/'beɪkəri/	....
ballroom (n)	/'bɔːlruːm/	....
bank (n)	/bæŋk/	....
birthday cake (n)	/'bɜːθdeɪ ˌkeɪk/	....
butcher's (n)	/'bʊtʃəz/	....
card shop (n)	/'kɑːd ʃɒp/	....
castle (n)	/'kɑːsl/	....
cathedral (n)	/kə'θiːdrəl/	....
changing room (n)	/'tʃeɪndʒɪŋ ˌruːm/	....
chemist's (n)	/'kemɪsts/	....
Christmas card (n)	/'krɪsməs ˌkɑːd/	....

Word	Phonetics	Translation
City Hall (n)	/ˌsɪti 'hɔːl/	....
clothes shop (n)	/'kləʊðz ʃɒp/	....
computer shop (n)	/kəm'pjuːtə ʃɒp/	....
concert hall (n)	/'kɒnsət ˌhɔːl/	....
congress hall (n)	/'kɒŋgres ˌhɔːl/	....
construction (n)	/kən'strʌkʃn/	....
dominate (v)	/'dɒmɪneɪt/	....
electrical store (n)	/ɪ'lektrɪkl ˌstɔː(r)/	....
exchange (v)	/ɪks'tʃeɪndʒ/	....
fit (v)	/fɪt/	....
fortune (n)	/'fɔːtjuːn/	....
government building (n)	/'gʌvənmənt ˌbɪldɪŋ/	....
grounds (n)	/graʊndz/	....
impressive (adj)	/ɪm'presɪv/	....
jeweller's (n)	/'dʒuːələz/	....
label (n)	/'leɪbl/	....
meat (n)	/miːt/	....
monument (n)	/'mɒnjəmənt/	....
museum (n)	/mju'ziːəm/	....
music shop (n)	/'mjuːzɪk ʃɒp/	....
newsagent's (n)	/'njuːzeɪdʒənts/	....
opera house (n)	/'ɒpərə ˌhaʊs/	....
palace (n)	/'pæləs/	....
paper (n)	/'peɪpə(r)/	....
parade (n)	/pə'reɪd/	....
pasta (n)	/'pæstə/	....
perfume (n)	/'pɜːfjuːm/	....
pick up (v)	/pɪk 'ʌp/	....
post office (n)	/'pəʊst ˌɒfɪs/	....
present (n)	/'preznt/	....
printer (n)	/'prɪntə(r)/	....
put away (v)	/pʊt ə'weɪ/	....
put on (v)	/pʊt 'ɒn/	....
receipt (n)	/rɪ'siːt/	....
residence (n)	/'rezɪdəns/	....
ring (n)	/rɪŋ/	....
sale (n)	/seɪl/	....
shoe shop (n)	/'ʃuː ʃɒp/	....
size (n)	/saɪz/	....

WORDLIST

Word	Phonetics	Translation
skyline (n)	/'skaɪlaɪn/	....
skyscraper (n)	/'skaɪskreɪpə(r)/	....
sports shop (n)	/'spɔːts ʃɒp/	....
stadium (n)	/'steɪdiəm/	....
stamp (n)	/stæmp/	....
statue (n)	/'stætjuː/	....
structure (n)	/'strʌktʃə(r)/	....
supermarket (n)	/'suːpəmɑːkɪt/	....
switch on (v)	/swɪtʃ 'ɒn/	....
symbolise (v)	/'sɪmbəlaɪz/	....
take off (v)	/teɪk 'ɒf/	....
temple (n)	/'templ/	....
tennis racquet (n)	/'tenɪs ˌrækɪt/	....
terrace (n)	/'terəs/	....
till (n)	/tɪl/	....
tower (n)	/'taʊə(r)/	....
traditionally (adv)	/trə'dɪʃənəli/	....
trainers (n)	/'treɪnəz/	....
turn down (v)	/tɜːn 'daʊn/	....
turn off (v)	/tɜːn 'ɒf/	....
turn on (v)	/tɜːn 'ɒn/	....

Get ready for your exam 5

Word	Phonetics	Translation
disco (n)	/'dɪskəʊ/	....
ice show (n)	/'aɪs ˌʃəʊ/	....
play (n)	/pleɪ/	....
rock concert (n)	/'rɒk ˌkɒnsət/	....

Get ready for your exam 6

Word	Phonetics	Translation
advantage (n)	/əd'vɑːntɪdʒ/	....
counter (n)	/'kaʊntə(r)/	....
customer (n)	/'kʌstəmə(r)/	....
disadvantage (n)	/ˌdɪsəd'vɑːntɪdʒ/	....
faulty (adj)	/'fɔːlti/	....

Unit 6 Technology

Word	Phonetics	Translation
addiction (n)	/ə'dɪkʃn/	....
calculator (n)	/'kælkjəleɪtə(r)/	....
camcorder (n)	/'kæmkɔːdə(r)/	....
CCTV camera (n)	/siː siː tiː 'viː ˌkæmrə(r)/	....
cure (v)	/kjʊə(r)/	....
damage (n)	/'dæmɪdʒ/	....
destroy (v)	/dɪ'strɔɪ/	....
digital radio (n)	/ˌdɪdʒɪtl 'reɪdiəʊ/	....
digital watch (n)	/ˌdɪdʒɪtl 'wɒtʃ/	....
DVD player (n)	/diː viː 'diː ˌpleɪə(r)/	....
enclose (v)	/ɪn'kləʊz/	....
entire (adj)	/ɪn'taɪə(r)/	....
environment (n)	/ɪn'vaɪrənmənt/	....
escalator (n)	/'eskəleɪtə(r)/	....
fantasy (n)	/'fæntəsi/	....
freezing (adj)	/'friːzɪŋ/	....
games console (n)	/'geɪmz ˌkɒnsəʊl/	....
grateful (adj)	/'greɪtfl/	....
hard disk recorder (n)	/hɑːd 'dɪsk rɪˌkɔːdə(r)/	....
inject (v)	/ɪn'dʒekt/	....
lift (n) (as in elevator)	/lɪft/	....
mobile phone (n)	/ˌməʊbaɪl 'fəʊn/	....
MP3 player (n)	/em piː 'θriː ˌpleɪə(r)/	....
nightmare (n)	/'naɪtmeə(r)/	....
nuclear weapon (n)	/ˌnjuːkliə 'wepn/	....
pick up (v)	/pɪk 'ʌp/	....
portable CD player (n)	/ˌpɔːtəbl siː 'diː ˌpleɪə(r)/	....
prediction (n)	/prɪ'dɪkʃn/	....
put away (v)	/pʊt ə'weɪ/	....
put down (v)	/pʊt 'daʊn/	....
put on (v)	/pʊt 'ɒn/	....
ringtone (n)	/'rɪŋtəʊn/	....
robot (n)	/'rəʊbɒt/	....
satellite TV (n)	/ˌsætəlaɪt tiː 'viː/	....
stereo (n)	/'steriəʊ/	....
submarine (n)	/sʌbmə'riːn/	....
switch on (v)	/swɪtʃ 'ɒn/	....
take off (v)	/teɪk 'ɒf/	....

WORDLIST

Word	Phonetics	Translation
take out (v)	/teɪk 'aʊt/	....
terrifying (adj)	/'terəfaɪɪŋ/	....
treatment (n)	/'triːtmənt/	....
turn down (v)	/tɜːn 'daʊn/	....
turn off (v)	/tɜːn 'ɒf/	....
turn on (v)	/tɜːn 'ɒn/	....
turn up (v)	/tɜːn 'ʌp/	....
video recorder (n)	/'vɪdiəʊ rɪˌkɔːdə(r)/	....
virus (n)	/'vaɪrəs/	....

Unit 7 Cultures and customs

Word	Phonetics	Translation
ban (n)	/bæn/	....
beckon (v)	/'bekn/	....
belch (v)	/beltʃ/	....
bend down (v)	/bend 'daʊn/	....
bow (v)	/baʊ/	....
bucket (n)	/'bʌkɪt/	....
casualty (n)	/'kæʒuəlti/	....
charity (n)	/'tʃærəti/	....
cheek (n)	/tʃiːk/	....
chopsticks (n)	/'tʃɒpstɪks/	....
compliment (n)	/'kɒmplɪmənt/	....
concerned (adj)	/kən'sɜːnd/	....
cross your legs (v)	/ˌkrɒs jə 'legz/	....
decline (v)	/dɪklaɪn/	....
escape (v)	/ɪ'skeɪp/	....
fold your arms (v)	/ˌfəʊld jər'ɑːmz/	....
hold hands (v)	/həʊld 'hændz/	....
hold out your arms (v)	/həʊld aʊt jər'ɑːmz/	....
horn (n)	/hɔːn/	....
host (n)	/həʊst/	....
hug (v)	/hʌg/	....
kiss (v)	/kɪs/	....
lie down (v)	/laɪ 'daʊn/	....
lift up your feet (v)	/lɪft ʌp jə 'fiːt/	....
nod (v)	/nɒd/	....
offensive (adj)	/ə'fensɪv/	....
participant (n)	/pɑː'tɪsɪpənt/	....
pat somebody on the back (v)	/ˌpæt sʌmbədi ɒn ðə 'bæk/	....

Word	Phonetics	Translation
point (v)	/pɔɪnt/	....
pointed (adj)	/'pɔɪntɪd/	....
protest (n)	/'prəʊtest/	....
punctuality (n)	/pʌŋktju'æləti/	....
put up your hand (v)	/pʊt ʌp jə 'hænd/	....
reduce (v)	/rɪ'djuːs/	....
(at) risk (n)	/ət 'rɪsk/	....
settler (n)	/'setlə(r)/	....
shake hands (v)	/ʃeɪk 'hændz/	....
shake your head (v)	/ˌʃeɪk jə 'hed/	....
sign up (v)	/saɪn 'ʌp/	....
sit down (v)	/sɪt 'daʊn/	....
sit up (v)	/sɪt 'ʌp/	....
stand up (v)	/stænd 'ʌp/	....
steep (adj)	/stiːp/	....
superstition (n)	/suːpə'stɪʃn/	....
turn over (v)	/tɜːn 'əʊvə(r)/	....
turn round (v)	/tɜːn 'raʊnd/	....
volunteer (v)	/vɒlən'tɪə(r)/	....
wave (v)	/weɪv/	....
wink (v)	/wɪŋk/	....
wish (n)	/wɪʃ/	....
wishbone (n)	/'wɪʃbəʊn/	....

Get ready for your exam 7

Word	Phonetics	Translation
dishwasher (n)	/'dɪʃwɒʃə(r)/	....
domestic appliance (n)	/dəˌmestɪk ə'plaɪəns/	....
freezer (n)	/'friːzə(r)/	....
fridge (n)	/frɪdʒ/	....
iron (n)	/'aɪən/	....
juicer (n)	/'dʒuːsə(r)/	....
kettle (n)	/'ketl/	....
microwave (n)	/'maɪkrəweɪv/	....
oven (n)	/'ʌvn/	....
toaster (n)	/'təʊstə(r)/	....
tumble dryer (n)	/ˌtʌmbl 'draɪə(r)/	....
vacuum cleaner (n)	/'vækjuːm ˌkliːnə(r)/	....
washing machine (n)	/'wɒʃɪŋ məˌʃiːn/	....

WORDLIST

Word	Phonetics	Translation	Word	Phonetics	Translation
Get ready for your exam 8			inform (v)	/ɪnˈfɔːm/	....
book (v)	/bʊk/	....	lava (n)	/ˈlɑːvə(r)/	....
bring (v)	/brɪŋ/	....	litter (n)	/ˈlɪtə(r)/	....
eat out (b)	/ˌiːt ˈaʊt/	....	oil (n)	/ɔɪl/	....
order (v)	/ˈɔːdə(r)/	....	optional (adj)	/ˈɒpʃənl/	....
pay (v)	/peɪ/	....	ozone layer (n)	/ˈəʊzəʊn ˌleɪə(r)/	....
			pesticide (n)	/ˈpestɪsaɪd/	....
Unit 8 What if ...?			petrol (n)	/ˈpetrəl/	....
act (v)	/ækt/	....	pick up (v)	/ˌpɪk ˈʌp/	....
apologise (v)	/əˈpɒlədʒaɪz/	....	pollute (v)	/pəˈluːt/	....
arms trade (n)	/ˈɑːmz treɪd/	....	pollution (n)	/pəˈluːʃn/	....
ash (n)	/æʃ/	....	poverty (n)	/ˈpɒvəti/	....
atmosphere (n)	/ˈætməsfɪə(r)/	....	predict (v)	/prɪˈdɪkt/	....
burn (v)	/bɜːn/	....	prediction (n)	/prɪˈdɪkʃn/	....
child labour (n)	/ˌtʃaɪld ˈleɪbə(r)/	....	pressure (n)	/ˈpreʃə(r)/	....
climate (n)	/ˈklaɪmət/	....	prize (n)	/praɪz/	....
coast (n)	/kəʊst/	....	produce (v)	/prəˈdjuːs/	....
collapse (v)	/kəˈlæps/	....	protect (v)	/prəˈtekt/	....
consume (v)	/kənˈsjuːm/	....	protection (n)	/prəˈtekʃn/	....
crater (n)	/ˈkreɪtə(r)/	....	public transport (n)	/ˈpʌblɪk ˈtrænspɔːt/	....
cross (adj)	/krɒs/	....	racism (n)	/ˈreɪsɪzm/	....
damage (n)	/ˈdæmɪdʒ/	....	reach (v)	/riːtʃ/	....
decompose (v)	/ˌdiːkəmˈpəʊz/	....	recycle (v)	/riːˈsaɪkl/	....
destroy (v)	/dɪˈstrɔɪ/	....	reduce (v)	/rɪˈdjuːs/	....
destruction (n)	/dɪˈstrʌkʃn/	....	renewable (adj)	/rɪˈnjuːəbl/	....
devastate (v)	/ˈdevəsteɪt/	....	rock (n)	/rɒk/	....
devastation (n)	/devəˈsteɪʃn/	....	sleeping bag (n)	/ˈsliːpɪŋ ˌbæg/	....
developing world (n)	/dɪˌveləpɪŋ ˈwɜːld/	....	suggest (v)	/səˈdʒest/	....
disease (n)	/dɪˈziːz/	....	sun burn (n)	/ˈsʌn bɜːn/	....
educate (v)	/ˈedʒukeɪt/	....	terrorism (n)	/ˈterərɪzm/	....
endangered species (n)	/ɪnˌdeɪndʒəd ˈspiːʃiz/	....	tsunami (n)	/tsuːˈnɑːmi/	....
erupt (v)	/ɪˈrʌpt/	....	vaccinate (v)	/ˈvæksɪneɪt/	....
eruption (n)	/ɪˈrʌpʃn/	....	volcano (n)	/vɒlˈkeɪnːəʊ/	....
famine (n)	/ˈfæmɪn/	....	war (n)	/wɔː(r)/	....
flooded (adj)	/ˈflʌdɪd/	....	warning (n)	/ˈwɔːnɪŋ/	....
global warming (n)	/ˌgləʊbl ˈwɔːmɪŋ/	....	wave (n)	/weɪv/	....
greenhouse gases (n)	/ˈgriːnhaʊs ˌgasɪz/	....			
homelessness (n)	/ˈhəʊmləsnəs/	....			
illegal (adj)	/ɪˈliːgl/	....			

WORDLIST

Word	Phonetics	Translation

Unit 9 Crime scene

Word	Phonetics	Translation
admit (v)	/əd'mɪt/	....
arrest (v)	/ə'rest/	....
astonished (adj)	/ə'stɒnɪʃt/	....
brilliant (adj)	/'brɪliənt/	....
burglary (n)	/'bɜːgləri/	....
canvas (n)	/'kænvəs/	....
catch (a criminal) (v)	/kætʃ/	....
catch up (v)	/kætʃ 'ʌp/	....
chaos (n)	/'keɪɒs/	....
charge (someone with a crime) (v)	/tʃɑːdʒ/	....
chase (v)	/tʃeɪs/	....
commit (a crime) (v)	/kə'mɪt/	....
computer virus (n)	/kəm'pjuːtə ˌvaɪrəs/	....
confess (v)	/kən'fes/	....
crime (n)	/kraɪm/	....
criminal (n)	/'krɪmɪnl/	....
detective (n)	/dɪ'tektɪv/	....
discover (v)	/dɪ'skʌvə(r)/	....
drug dealer (n)	/'drʌg ˌdiːlə(r)/	....
drug dealing (n)	/'drʌg ˌdiːlɪŋ/	....
guilty (adj)	/'gɪlti/	....
gun (n)	/gʌn/	....
joyrider (n)	/'dʒɔɪraɪdə(r)/	....
joyriding (n)	/'dʒɔɪraɪdɪŋ/	....
murder (n)	/'mɜːdə(r)/	....
murderer (n)	/'mɜːdərə(r)/	....
order (v)	/'ɔːdə(r)/	....
prison (n)	/'prɪzn/	....
question (v)	/'kwestʃn/	....
realise (v)	/'riːəlaɪz/	....
reward (n)	/rɪ'wɔːd/	....
robber (n)	/'rɒbə(r)/	....
robbery (n)	/'rɒbəri/	....
satellite navigation system (n)	/ˌsætəlaɪt nævɪ'geɪʃn ˌsɪstəm/	....
shoplifter (n)	/'ʃɒplɪftə(r)/	....
shoplifting (n)	/'ʃɒplɪftɪŋ/	....
suspended sentence (n)	/sə,spendɪd 'sentəns/	....
terrific (adj)	/tə'rɪfɪk/	....
terrified (adj)	/'terɪfaɪd/	....
theft (n)	/θeft/	....
trial (n)	/'traɪəl/	....
vandal (n)	/'vændl/	....
vandalism (n)	/'vændəlɪzm/	....
victim (n)	/'vɪktɪm/	....
vital (adj)	/'vaɪtl/	....

Get ready for your exam 9

Word	Phonetics	Translation
cave (n)	/keɪv/	....
crops (n)	/krɒps/	....
drought (n)	/draʊt/	....
drown (v)	/draʊn/	....
earthquake (n)	/'ɜːθkweɪk/	....
flood (n)	/flʌd/	....
flood (v)	/flʌd/	....
forest (n)	/'fɒrɪst/	....
forest fire (n)	/ˌfɒrɪst 'faɪə(r)/	....
grow (v)	/grəʊ/	....
hurricane (n)	/'hʌrɪkeɪn/	....
island (n)	/'aɪlənd/	....
lake (n)	/leɪk/	....
mountain (n)	/'maʊntən/	....
rise (v)	/raɪz/	....
ruin (v)	/'ruːɪn/	....
sand dune (n)	/'sænd djuːn/	....
starve (v)	/stɑːv/	....
storm (n)	/stɔːm/	....
tornado (n)	/tɔː'neɪdəʊ/	....
tsunami (n)	/tsuː'nɑːmi/	....
volcanic eruption (n)	/vɒlˌkænɪk ɪ'rʌpʃn/	....

Get ready for your exam 10

Word	Phonetics	Translation
cell (n)	/sel/	....
lonely (adj)	/'ləʊnli/	....
prison (n)	/'prɪzn/	....
prisoner (n)	/'prɪznə(r)/	....
punish (v)	/'pʌnɪʃ/	....
visitor (n)	/'vɪzɪtə(r)/	....

WORDLIST

Word	Phonetics	Translation

Unit 10 The written word

Word	Phonetics	Translation
accuracy (n)	/'ækjərəsi/	....
atlas (n)	/'ætləs/	....
autobiography (n)	/ˌɔːtəbaɪ'ɒgrəfi/	....
back cover (n)	/ˌbæk 'kʌvə(r)/	....
badge (n)	/bædʒ/	....
base on (v)	/'beɪs ɒn/	....
be set in (v)	/biː 'set ɪn/	....
best-seller (n)	/ˌbest 'selə(r)/	....
biography (n)	/baɪ'ɒgrəfi/	....
chapter (n)	/'tʃæptə(r)/	....
character (n)	/'kærəktə(r)/	....
classic novel (n)	/'klæsɪk 'nɒvl/	....
comic (n)	/'kɒmɪk/	....
comic novel (n)	/'kɒmɪk 'nɒvl/	....
contents page (n)	/'kɒntents ˌpeɪdʒ/	....
cookbook (n)	/'kʊkbʊk/	....
criticism (n)	/'krɪtɪsɪzm/	....
dictionary (n)	/'dɪkʃnri/	....
disciplined (adj)	/'dɪsɪplɪnd/	....
encyclopaedia (n)	/ɪnˌsaɪklə'piːdiə/	....
fantasy (n)	/'fæntəsi/	....
fiction (n)	/'fɪkʃn/	....
front cover (n)	/ˌfrʌnt 'kʌvə(r)/	....
gripping (adj)	/'grɪpɪŋ/	....
guidebook (n)	/'gaɪdbʊk/	....
hardback (n)	/'hɑːdbæk/	....
historical novel (n)	/hɪ'stɒrɪkl 'nɒvl/	....
horror (n)	/'hɒrə(r)/	....
humble (adj)	/'hʌmbl/	....
identify with (v)	/aɪ'dentɪfaɪ wɪð/	....
imaginary (adj)	/ɪ'mædʒɪnəri/	....
intend (v)	/ɪn'tend/	....
issue (n)	/'ɪʃuː/	....
kidnap (v)	/'kɪdnæp/	....
literature (n)	/'lɪtrətʃə(r)/	....
magazine (n)	/mægə'ziːn/	....
manual (n)	/'mænjuəl/	....
newspaper (n)	/'njuːspeɪpə(r)/	....
novel (n)	/'nɒvl/	....
novelist (n)	/'nɒvəlɪst/	....
paperback (n)	/'peɪpəbæk/	....
perform (v)	/pə'fɔːm/	....
persistent (adj)	/pə'sɪstənt/	....
play (n)	/pleɪ/	....
playwright (n)	/'pleɪraɪt/	....
poem (n)	/'pəʊɪm/	....
poet (n)	/'pəʊɪt/	....
print (v)	/prɪnt/	....
publication (n)	/pʌblɪ'keɪʃn/	....
publish (v)	/'pʌblɪʃ/	....
quality (n)	/'kwɒləti/	....
recommend (v)	/rekə'mend/	....
retire (v)	/rɪ'taɪə(r)/	....
romantic fiction (n)	/rəʊˌmæntɪk 'fɪkʃn/	....
science fiction (n)	/ˌsaɪəns 'fɪkʃn/	....
short story (n)	/ˌʃɔːt 'stɔːri/	....
spine (n)	/spaɪn/	....
telepathy (n)	/tə'lepəθi/	....
textbook (n)	/'tekstbʊk/	....
thought-provoking (adj)	/'θɔːt prəˌvəʊkɪŋ/	....
title (n)	/'taɪtl/	....
translate (v)	/trænz'leɪt/	....

IRREGULAR VERBS

Base form	Past simple	Past participle
be	was/were	been
become	became	become
begin	began	begun
bend	bent	bent
bite	bit	bitten
blow	blew	blown
break	broke	broken
bring	brought	brought
build	built	built
burn	burnt	burnt
buy	bought	bought
can	could	been able to
catch	caught	caught
choose	chose	chosen
come	came	come
cost	cost	cost
cut	cut	cut
do	did	done
draw	drew	drawn
drink	drank	drunk
drive	drove	driven
eat	ate	eaten
fall	fell	fallen
feel	felt	felt
fight	fought	fought
find	found	found
fly	flew	flown
forget	forgot	forgotten
get	got	got
give	gave	given
go	went	gone
grow	grew	grown
hang	hung	hung
have	had	had
hear	heard	heard
hide	hid	hidden
hit	hit	hit
keep	kept	kept
know	knew	known
lay	laid	laid
lead	led	led
learn	learnt/-ed	learnt/-ed
leave	left	left
lend	lent	lent
lose	lost	lost

Base form	Past simple	Past participle
make	made	made
mean	meant	meant
meet	met	met
overcome	overcame	overcome
pay	paid	paid
put	put	put
read	read	read
ride	rode	ridden
ring	rang	rung
run	ran	run
say	said	said
see	saw	seen
sell	sold	sold
send	sent	sent
set	set	set
shake	shook	shaken
shine	shone	shone
shoot	shot	shot
show	showed	shown/-ed
shut	shut	shut
sing	sang	sung
sink	sank	sunk
sit	sat	sat
sleep	slept	slept
smell	smelt/-ed	smelt/-ed
speak	spoke	spoken
spell	spelt/-ed	spelt/-ed
spend	spent	spent
spill	spilt/-ed	spilt/-ed
stand	stood	stood
steal	stole	stolen
swim	swam	swum
take	took	taken
teach	taught	taught
tell	told	told
think	thought	thought
throw	threw	thrown
understand	understood	understood
wake	woke	woken
wear	wore	worn
win	won	won
write	wrote	written